Garden of Life
a poetic awakening
by Jaya Kamlani

**Editor & Designer
Minal Kamlani**

Copyright © Jaya Kamlani
All rights reserved
First Published 2015
Republished 2021
Kindle Direct Publishing
US Library of Congress
Washington D.C., USA
ISBN: 1508610177
ISBN 13: 978-1508610175
Library of Congress Control Number: 2015903244

No part of this book may be reproduced in any print or digital form, or stored on any information storage device. Fair use permitted to quote a passage from the book, provided this book is mentioned as a reference source.

Introduction

Garden of Life is an enchanting collection of thought-provoking poems set in different parts of the world: about great legends and dreams, war (real wars) and peace, nature scenes, inspiration, personal transformation, Covid-19, and what happened to America in 2020. Legends such as the life and teachings of the first Buddha, and tales of the young Egyptian King, Tutankhamen.

Our beautiful world has been torn apart by wars, hate, violence, and Covid-19. It needs healing. Despite our different faiths, cultures, and geographies, despite our politics, we must rise together in love and peace.

Jaya Kamlani is an award-winning Indian American author, poet, and Global Goodwill Ambassador. She uses storytelling to encourage introspection of how our actions impact humanity. As a former Silicon Valley business and information technology consultant, she is a firm believer in *kaizen*—continuous improvement—be it in manufacturing, business, or ourselves. Graduate of St. Xavier's College, Mumbai, India, she has been living in America since 1969.

Her literary works include non-fiction *To India, with Tough Love* (2013); memoir *Scent of Yesterday* (2014); poetry collection *Garden of Life* (2015/21); non-fiction *The Conspirators: Taking Down The President* (2020); and upcoming sequel *The Conspirators 2*.

Kamlani has received several gold awards for literature from the Government of India: Hind Rattan (Jewel of India), Mahatma Gandhi Samman, Nav Rattan (one of 9 jewels), two Bharat Samman (Pride of India) awards and the Bharat Shiromani (Crest Jewel of India) Award. More at: www.jayakamlani.com

Garden of Life
Poems by Jaya Kamlani

Introduction
Bedtime Stories

Without You	2
Kami Gods	4
Chinese Matchmaker	6
Garden of Life	8
Grandma's Tin Box	10
Poor Henry Chandler	13
In Search of Utopia	14
Mystery Envelope	16
Murphy's Clouds	17
A Farm Song	18
The Tribal Doctor	20
Tutankhamen	22
Sleep Thumbelina, Sleep	25
Everything Will Be OK	26

Alchemy   27

A Distant Voice	28
Christmas Gift	30
Thin-Skinned	31
Divine Scale	32
Seven Year Itch	34
Journey	35
Narcissist	36
Puffs	37
A Rewarding Life	38
The Salt March	40
The First Buddha	42
Never Too Old To Dream	46

War & Peace   *47*

    Woodstock & War   48
    The Great American Tragedy   50
    Ravages of War   52
    Papa, Make Bad War Go Away   54
    Don't Cry Wolf   55
    Bury Your Weapons   56
    Enemy Within   57
    Eye For An Eye   58
    Stain on American Tapestry   60
    A New Tomorrow   62
    Rise America, Rise   63
    Live Life   64

Red, White & The Blues   *65*

    A Soldier's Story   66
    Love & Soup Kitchen   68
    Hungry in New York City   70
    A Ray of Sunshine   72
    Living High On Wall Street   74
    The Gambler   75
    On Death Row   76

Stolen Childhood   *83*

    Jaws of Hell   84
    Flying Trapeze   85
    Escape from Fate   86
    Trail of Tears   88
    Blood Diamonds   90

Reflecting Pool   *91*
    Curio Cabinet   92

Those Good Old Days	96
Ode to My Brother	98
The Roads I Traveled	99
Don't Let Life Pass You By	100
Pearls of Life	101
Footprints in the Sand	102
Field of Shamrocks	104
House of Light	105

Our Beautiful World — *107*

Sunset at Goa Beach	108
The Waves	110
Summer in The Adirondacks	111
As The Seasons Turn	112
God's Palette	114
Snake Plant	115
A World Without Art	116
Dying River	118
A Bird's Call	119
Come Dance With Me	120
Torch of Harmony	122

America 2020 — *123*

The Invisible Enemy, Covid-19	124
Summer of Riots	130
Tyranny, Be Not Proud	138

Notes — **140**

Bedtime Stories

Garden Of Life

Without You

She was a bit on the wild side,
could babble all the way
to Babylonia;
he was well-bred,
soft-spoken, a man of few words,
loved to spend his time reading;
when the two first met
at the local library,
sparks flew
and lit up the room.
She was a social butterfly,
vivacious, a bit spendthrift,
loved her man dearly,
gave him good advice,
made sure he took his vitamins.
He was an academic, a minimalist,
for he had seen hardship,

Garden Of Life

but never skimped on her,
for she got him flattering sweaters,
and baked his favorite walnut brownies.
She was an aspiring photographer,
well read, and no dummy,
maintained his stock portfolio,
and humored him with her zany wit:
Add a little swagger to your walk, honey,
strut into the room as if you are The Duke.
He would then put down his book,
take off his rimless glasses,
hold her in his arms and say:
What would I do without you?
Thus, the two lived happily ever after,
each complimenting the other,
yet, never in competition
with each other.

Garden Of Life

Kami Gods

Akiko jumped out of bed this morning from the earth tremors,
put on his slippers, robe and glasses, got his family together;

rushed to the street, found the city of Kobe in total turmoil:
caved streets, buckled bridges, raging fires, wailing sirens;

walked a mile, broke down to find his general store in ruins,
quake had crippled his town: death, devastation everywhere;

distressed, Akiko and wife visited a Shinto shrine, to invoke
spirits of the Kami gods wafting over trees, streams and rocks.

walked past the orange Torii gate, up a white pebble path,
to a Japanese Zen garden of Bonsai and flowering shrubs.

Copper wind chimes sashayed, kept the evil spirits at bay,
as they ambled down to a white lotus pond, lost in thoughts.

Before entering the shrine, Akiko and wife purified themselves
with holy water flowing from a dragonhead into a large basin.

Garden Of Life

Scooping water with a ladle, he rinsed his mouth and hands,
felt pangs of guilt for not having visited the temple for long.

Two fox statues guarded entrance to the gabled-roof shrine,
Buddhist chants echoed, Akiko lit candles in the brass lanterns.

He bowed, rang the temple bell, clapped hands, bowed again,
each dropped five yen in the offering box and made a wish.

In return, the temple custodian gave them each a fortune slip.
Akiko read the *omikuji*, tied it to a pine post – it was not good.

From an amulet stall on the temple grounds, they bought two
omamori good luck charms and wore them around their necks.

A year later, still no luck, they moved out of their Kobe home,
bought a small flat in Tokyo, nearby opened a hardware store.

In two years business improved, they went to thank the gods,
read his fortune slip and took it home – this time it was good.

Chinese Matchmaker

In the coastal town of Shenzhen, lived an old matchmaker,
Chung's mother visited her, sought a nice girl for her son;

matchmaker suggested three girls living in a nearby town,
mother met with the three, wasted no time to size them up;

first girl was pretty, but with a limp could not help her son,
the second was smart, but did not smile, that was troubling;

third was pretty, smart and gracious, it pleased the mother,
matchmaker took boy and girl's birthdates to a fortune teller;

dates did not match, another bride was selected for Chung,
a favorable wedding day was set, per the Chinese calendar;

the two took to each other, he brought her roses and mirth,
they went to movies, beautiful gardens, music performances.

Garden Of Life

soon Korean War broke, Communist Party backed the North,
Chung's mother wanted son to marry, before he went to war;

Chung and Ruan were wed in haste by the town's magistrate,
Chinese Communist Party Chief was witness at civil ceremony;

no exchange of betrothal gifts, no red sedan chair for bride,
no band serenaded the couple, no celebration with friends;

Chung sported a Lenin jacket and a red sash across his chest,
Ruan in red, mirror locket around her neck, to ward off evil;

Chung was sent to war, wrote home once, never returned,
another victim of Korean War, of the Mao Tse-tung regime;

Ruan blessed with a baby boy, sadly she died in childbirth,
it was an ominous year of the Tiger when the two had wed.

Garden of Life

In the distant hills of Texas, lived a little girl named Laura,
as an autistic child, she attended a special needs school;
when she came home, she had milk and some snacks,
then went to the garden to see her favorite yellow rose.

Red robins flew to the birdfeeder and nibbled on seeds,
then sat on a fence and sang sweetly tweet-tweet-tweet,
as they watched her sniff and kiss the lovely yellow rose,
and play with her black Labrador, she simply adored.

Despite her handicap, Laura was a delightful gifted child,
she drew spirited pictures of her dog playing in the yard,
hummingbirds sapping on a rose bush, blue jays singing,
ladybugs on leaves, cuckoos with worms in their beaks.

When the sun eased down, birds returned to their nests,
flew back another day to hear her sing, prance and play;
she slipped wilted petals between the leaves of her books,
but how her eyes gleamed to see her yellow rose bloom.

Garden Of Life

One day, her mother took her to Capital of Texas Zoo,
where lemur monkeys with beady eyes and striped tails
delighted her as they leapt and frolicked on the grounds.
Laura was happy playing with the birds and butterflies.

All at once, her eyes were drawn to a white peacock,
that struck a majestic pose, flaunting wide its feathers;
while its blue-coated cousins gathered and juxtaposed.
Next day, she spent hours sketching pretty peacocks.

The rose thrived that summer, as if by some magic spell,
until one day, when gale winds blew and it got tart cold,
the yellow rose fell off the bush with a gust and withered;
she picked it up, kissed it and buried it with a sweet song.

Year after year, the rose bush's bloom brought her cheer,
as she sat on a swing by an old oak tree and sang merrily;
then the snails, ladybugs, caterpillars crept out of the dirt,
birds chirped, butterflies fluttered, the Lab spun in circles.

Grandma's Tin Box

In an upscale community of Barcelona, Spain,
lived a bashful seven-year old named Miguel;
one afternoon as he stepped off the school bus,
he found two shiny silver coins down the road.

He picked them up and put them in his pocket,
showed to Grandma that evening after dinner;
she handed him a tin box to save all his money,
added a few coins of her own to his collection.

When his uncle gave him a pocketful of silver,
he rushed to Grandma, showed her the money;
she told him: Put them in your tin box, Miguel,
then someday you can buy yourself big bicycle.

For his eighth birthday, the little boy received
a few toy cars, fancy clothes and paper money;
he showed all his gifts to Grandma, who said:
Save all your money in your tin box, Miguel.

Poor Miguel was so confused, "Grandma, you
always tell me to put the money in the tin box,
but I want to buy toys with the paper money."
Save it for bigger toys this Christmas, she said.

Garden Of Life

Come Christmas, Grandma told her grandson:
Miguel, we're going out today. Bring all your
toys in a big bag and the tin box along with you.
The little boy wondered where they were going.

They drove past tall palms and Gaudi buildings,
then pulled up in an impoverished area of town.
Grandma asked the driver to gather the children,
who rushed to the car, the mothers behind them.

Stroking the lad's face with affection, she said,
Miguel, now give each child a toy from the bag;
although heartbroken, the little boy did as told,
with all his toys gone, he tossed the empty sack.

Grandma then asked him to empty the tin box,
give his money to the poor children's mothers;
Miguel, now in tears, clung tight to his tin box,
putting his other arm around grandma, he cried.

Miguel, on Christmas Day we must do charity,
make other people's lives also happy, she said,
as she pulled a stack of money from her purse,
and the two gave freely to the less fortunate.

Garden Of Life

Grandma, woman of old grace and fine taste,
then directed the driver to the famed Cathedral,
there, slipped some money into a donation box,
lit a candle, down on her knees, thanked God.

They drove to the large toy store in Barcelona,
to buy her grandson a bike and some toy cars;
brimming with joy, Miguel hugged grandma,
who kissed him and shared pearls of wisdom.

When you give, give freely, with love and joy,
and your room will be filled with plenty of toys;
empty your hands before you can receive, son.
Thus, the little lad learned to give and to share.

She took him to the park and the sandy beaches,
he frolicked in the waters, then built sandcastles.
Miguel, who lost his parents in an auto accident,
was the darling and sunshine of Grandma's life.

When he turned eighteen, she bought him a car,
so he could drive to college and take his girl out,
he was well balanced, for she had raised him well,
fared well in school, had a good circle of friends.

Garden Of Life

Poor Henry Chandler

Henry Chandler's father was a doctor, so was his grandfather.
he often heard them tell inspiring stories of their alma mater;
in keeping with tradition, he enrolled at the same university,
burned candles at both ends, but felt a sense of inadequacy.

He hailed from a wealthy family, hardships he had seen none,
upon graduating from medical school, told he was a fine son;
compassionate and giving, he had funded his friend's tuition,
following residency, hoped he would make a fine physician.

After a grueling day at work, he came home, grabbed a beer,
watched his favorite comedy show to bring him some cheer;
made himself a sandwich, read for a while, then hit the sack,
eighty-hour workweeks sometimes gave him a panic attack.

Sleep-deprived, he worried over making a wrong diagnosis,
hoped to remember difference between sclerosis and fibrosis;
he recalled a day when internship drove his friend to suicide,
it was a sad day when something deep inside him also died.

He was reminded of an intern, who collapsed in the elevator,
the time a patient was operated on the wrong leg by a doctor;
he reminisced over Emma, the nurse who gave him a neck rub,
asked her out many times, but she did not like his boy's club.

Poor Henry Chandler, could not convince a girl he loved her,
they rode in his red Morgan, but did not want to be his lover;
despite his fame and fortune, Henry had no steady girlfriend,
he grew old and lonesome, looking for love at every bend.

Garden Of Life

In Search of Utopia

Demetrius looked out his window this morning, deep in thought, felt a numbing void in life, despite his budding career in finance; by the window sat a wide cabinet lined with a collection of books of Plato, Dostoyevsky, Nietzsche, Lao Tzu, Descartes, Einstein…

Feeling restless, he went to a bookstore, there ran into Anastasia, an old friend from his philosophy class at the Oxford University; they got cheese, baklava, bottle of ouzo and walked to his place, chatted about Thomas More's imaginary happy island, Utopia.

Demetrius steered the dialogue to the great philosopher, Socrates; Greeks in long hair came to hear him talk of values and democracy, he told them not to fight the old system, build a new one instead, was arrested for corrupting the young and given hemlock to drink.

They discussed Plato's Republic — Everyone has a role in society: educated govern, soldiers defend, farmers and artisans produce; they discussed Aristotle's code of ethics and his rational analysis, he believed the universe has no beginning; it shall have no end.

Reflecting on Zen, Anna took a big swig of ouzo and rambled on, Zen is here and now, living in the moment, being close to nature, body and mind working as one, it is self-awareness, selflessness. Demetrius, I am awakened. I am enlightened. . . I am in ZAZEN.

Demetrius rushed to the kitchen for more cheese and crackers, handed the plate to Anna, who was by now in such a delirium; while he prepared warm tea laced with a tangy twist of lemon, he recalled how he once carried a torch for her, then lost her.

Garden Of Life

She sipped on tea while he leafed through Robert Pirsig's book, Zen and the Art of Motorcycle Maintenance, read about how yesterday's wisdom can co-exist with today's technology, but after a revolution, the old regime thoughts must be put to bed.

They ordered in Chinese dinner, cracked open fortune cookies, read wise Confucius: "Wherever you go, go with all your heart," "Life is really simple, but we insist on making it complicated." Ah! What would fortune cookies be without Confucius wisdom?

They debated what would happen if government banned books, or firemen burned them, as in Ray Bradbury's Fahrenheit 451. Those in power don't like free thinkers, they fear losing control if people read books, are well informed, and learned the truth.

Alas Demeet, you're right, Socrates was way ahead of his time, we need true democracy, not some dystopian crisis of despair; for long, special interest groups and big corporations dictated, then the people revolted, took control of their future at the polls.

Cited Einstein on war: In two weeks the sheep-like masses of any country can be worked up by the newspapers into such a state of excited fury that men are prepared to put on uniforms and kill and be killed, for the sake of the sordid ends of a few interested parties.

They mused over their own Utopian vision: a world where people come together, make music and dance, a river runs through town, nearby a bookstore, cafés, shops. . . then Demetrius put on music, took Anna into his arms and the two danced softly into the night.

Mystery Envelope

A lady walks into an upscale bar,
in stilettos and red polkadot scarf,
carrying a bulky brown envelope
under her arm, she looks around.

A man with a French beard winks,
cannot part his eyes from her hips,
she talks to a man in a Russian hat,
he's well heeled, wore an eyepatch.

He orders a martini, she some wine,
they share a few laughs, he departs,
the lady gulps down the Cabernet,
calls the waiter and orders another.

Frenchie gingerly approaches her,
joins her for chat over glass of wine,
notices the brown envelope is gone,
muses if the Russian is a private eye.

Scarlett's her name, spying her game,
she flirts, she pries, she asks Frenchie
to join her on an exotic island escape,
but he's not lured by her proposition.

Murphy's Clouds

Yet another day, Murphy's Law prevailed,
Anything that can go wrong, will, he said,
virus attack snuck past my laptop firewall,
dishwasher decided to skip the final rinse.

Phone rang, turned out to be a prank call,
he huffed and puffed, so I unplugged him,
credit card bill had charges I did not incur,
neighbor's dog barked until my head hurt.

As sunshine broke through Murphy's clouds,
I sat in the balcony overlooking a jade pool,
sipped on lemonade and wrote a few verses,
and hummed along to my old favorite tunes.

A rainbow appeared in a spectrum of colors,
met an old friend for chat, laughs, and drinks,
drove home re-energized and in good cheer,
as Balsamic Moon morphed to a New Moon.

A Farm Song

Chotu, the old farmer, was troubled over his crop yield,
last year, the rains had washed away his five-acre field,
the loan shark came and carted away his two buffaloes;
this year the rains were late and ruined all his tomatoes.

Deep in debt, the farmers of Vidarbha committed suicide,
they hanged themselves or drank lethal dose of pesticide,
another jumped in the nearby Indian river and drowned,
some sold their land, in search of jobs, were city-bound.

It troubled Chotu to see his children go hungry and cry,
he pumped water from his well, until the spring ran dry,
few seeds sprouted but wilted away, drought was severe,
so he sold his favorite goat that gave milk year after year.

Every night, he lit oil lamps and incense of sandalwood,
offered flowers to rain goddess Indra, sweets, and food,
clasping his hands, heavy-hearted he chanted in despair:
our children are hungry, land parched and pantries bare.

When the village money lender came to collect his dues,
Chotu pleaded on his knees, beleaguered by the blues:
Sahib, please, in two months I promise to settle my debt.
Lender scoffed: Your land shall soon be mine, you forget.

Garden Of Life

The sneer of the loan shark reached the ears of the gods,
the clouds roared, and the sky lit up with lightning rods,
raindrops pitter-pattered on the red roof and the treetop,
children danced and sang, and the rains would not stop.

Next morning, Chotu returned to his rain-soaked field,
sang praises of the rain gods, hoped for a generous yield,
with sickle and spade they heaved and hoed until sunset,
worried no more about the loan shark or his nasty threat.

Chotu's farm yielded bounty of vegetables row after row,
a burly farmer next door, let the grass on his land grow,
packed bales of hay, sold them to farmers for cattle feed,
another did well with his corn and millets reusable seed.

One night of the harvest festival, Chotu lit a big bonfire,
celebrated with farmer friends, dressed in colorful attire,
they danced, sang the farm song, broke bread together,
pledged to install drip irrigation, not rely on the weather.

From his bounty, he saved money to put in a drip system,
now he had time to see his farm through a different prism,
no more threats by loan sharks, no more pangs of hunger,
he saved money for a bigger barn, bought some lumber.

Garden Of Life

The Tribal Doctor

Three decades ago, in the Biligiriranga Hills of India,
a doctor arrived to provide care for the Soliga tribe,
but when he got there, the southern village was bare,
fearful of outsiders, they went and hid in the woods.

The doctor did not lose heart, he had come to stay,
he set up a clinic at a shack, soon the patients came,
with illness, worm infestation, injuries from tree falls,
allergies, snake bites, wild-boar and bison attacks.

He doubled his one-room day-clinic as a night school,
soon the shack gave way to a ten-bed hospital room,
a school was built on a large plot, and children learned
not from texts, but from stories, games, experiments.

But after the midday meal at school, the little darlings
wandered off into the woods, climbed trees, took naps,
refused discipline, so other students were hauled in on
bullock carts, or carried on backs from nearby hamlets.

Garden Of Life

Tribals then acquired livelihood skills: dairy farming,
fishing, basket-weaving, food processing and sewing;
they built homes, roads, brought in water and energy,
in an alcohol-and-communist-free zone of B.R. Hills.

Long before doctor's arrival, tribals had signed away
land rights to a robber baron, who reaped a big bounty
from fruit of tamarind trees, paid pittance for their toil;
doctor protested with the tribals to reclaim land rights.

Doctor jailed, refused to apply for bail, two days later
he was freed, and the Soliga tribe liberated from illegal
bonded labor, with the land rights settled in their favor;
no more would they fear mining or razing of their land.

***

*All the wealth of the world cannot help one little village
if the people are not taught to help themselves.*
— Swami Vivekananda

Tutankhamen

One afternoon, when the sun hid
behind the clouds,
raindrops drummed down
like gumdrops from heaven,
I prepared hot chocolate
with marshmallows for my little ones,
kindled a fire log,
then sat by the warm flames
with our German Shepherd, and
read them a book about Egypt's King Tut.

The children sipped on their drinks,
and lent me their ears,
as I leafed through the legend of
King Tut, crowned at nine,
buried at eighteen,
in the Valley of the Kings,
a valley of the dead.
How did he die? asked my little son,
rapt by the magic of the fable.
From a head injury, I replied.

Garden Of Life

Where is the Valley of the Kings?
Far in the desert, to my little girl I said,
in a town called Thebes,
by the River Nile,
where tombs of ancient pharaohs lie;
people of Egypt mourned his death,
they rubbed him down with oil,
wrapped him like a mummy,
and placed him gently
in a fancy casket.

Why rub him with oil? asked my son,
as a feisty thunderclap
sent a shiver through him.
So his body would not rot or smell, I replied.
They placed a gold mask on his face,
sealed his coffin,
on it, painted his face.
Why? asked my curious munchkins.
So people could tell
who was buried inside, I replied.

Garden Of Life

They laid his casket in a burial tomb,
filled it with treasures in its four rooms,
built a pyramid over it.
Treasures! What treasures?
Gold throne, furniture, fancy clothes,
jewelry, pottery, food, even seven magic oars.
Why food? He was dead, said my little one.
So when the king woke up,
he would eat and ferry across
the River Nile, I replied.

How could he wake up if he was dead?
As the rain beat on the window pane,
to my children I explained
the mysteries of afterlife;
people of Egypt believed,
the king's soul would one day return,
find the casket with his painted face,
and quietly enter his frame,
then King Tut of Egypt
would come to life again.

The fire crackled in blue and amber,
as I read to my children the legend
of the young king of Egypt,
Tutankhamen.

Garden Of Life

Sleep Thumbelina, Sleep

Sweet Thumbelina, sleep,
the sun has gone to bed,
the moon glides along,
till night morphs to dawn;
the sheep are in the pen,
the cows are in the barn,
the horses in their stables,
night owl keeps a watch;
Sweet Thumbelina, sleep,
while I hum a sweet song,
the birds are in their nests,
the angels keep you warm;
nana has gone to paradise,
let us send her valentines;
do not weep my little one,
the heart will mend in time.
Sweet Thumbelina, sleep,
while I hum a sweet song;
Sunday, we go to the park,
feed duckies some bread;
for your birthday this year,
I shall get you a little pup,
to play with all year long,
Sweet Thumbelina, sleep,
the sheep are in the pen,
the cows are in the barn,
the sun has gone to bed,
the moon glides along.

Everything Will Be OK

Dear God, you made this world so beautiful,
you gave us humming streams and songbirds,
I feel your presence when I hear wind-chimes,
I see you walking down the field of daffodils.

Some may doubt you or even lose faith in you,
no, not me, for you blessed me with patience;
driving down the street, when I saw a big sign:
Everything will be OK – I was reminded of you.

Then one day, the mystic barn sign was gone,
in its place a mural of gold field and butterflies,
dear sweet Lord, although I miss that barn sign,
I now see you walking down that field of gold.

When storm clouds hover and there is despair,
I do so remind myself… *Everything will be OK.*

Alchemy

Garden Of Life

A Distant Voice

A young man jogged along a nature trail when
he came upon a fork and took a turn,
wondered where the path led.
a distant voice whispered:
Follow the light.
*

He walked the dirt trail for a few hundred feet,
saw a bright light illume a small pond,
wondered where the light led.
The voice whispered:
Go to the cottage.
*

He walked down the track by an old oak tree,
saw a cottage with a white picket fence,
wondered who lived there.
The voice whispered:
Go inside.
*

The door was ajar, still he knocked three times,
no answer, knocked again and went in;
a pale old man lay on the floor.
The voice whispered:
Seek help.
*

Jogger picked up the phone, but line was dead,
he fetched the car keys from the table,
carried the old man to his car.
The voice whispered:
Hurry, son.
*

Garden Of Life

To a nearby hospital he drove as fast as he could,
learned that the man had suffered a stroke;
next day, he went to check on him.
The voice whispered:
You did fine, son.

*

The old man's family thanked the jogger for help,
took father home to live with them,
asked jogger to stay in touch.
The voice whispered:
Your new kin.

*

That Christmas, he was invited by the man's family,
they took to him like one of their own,
such love not seen in his home.
The voice whispered:
Next Christmas.

*

He visited his newfound family the next Christmas,
shared Yule tide greetings, exchanged gifts,
heard stories of bygone holidays;
The voice whispered,
Bid Goodbye.

*

A month later, he received a call, the old man was dead,
jogger treasured their last days together,
words of wisdom he had learned.
The distant voice whispered,
You're a noble man.

*

Garden Of Life

Christmas Gift

There lived a woman in Ohio, widowed early at forty,
She worked from dawn to dusk, to keep from poverty.
Through all the striving years, she kept herself warm,
Lit candles at both ends through the relentless storm.

One day, she found new love as she walked in the park,
Kept her lips sealed so chatty neighbors would not talk.
Went to church on Sunday in a fancy hat with feathers,
He walked in, slid in the pew, slipped his hand in hers.

She strode with spring in her step and glow on her face,
Friends remarked she looked radiant in pretty blue lace.
She blushed when they said she had aged like fine wine,
Amused, she replied, I must have mellowed with time.

One day when she drove into town, the smile left her face,
Alas, she found her old man in a young woman's embrace.
So for Christmas she got herself a playful little Shitsu dog,
The pup snuggled by the fireplace, she kindled a Yule log.

Thin-Skinned

This old man was very thin-skinned,
    every scoff, every rebuke,
    every slap on his wrist,
unleashed a stream of tears of crushing silence.

Soon he learned to dodge and bob,
    sing Bee-Bop-A-Lula,
    twist, cha-cha and rock,
until life's punches knocked again at his door.

Slowly the knockings took their toll,
    rid hardiness he had grown,
    years wore, he became sore,
thin-skinned the old man became once more.

Divine Scale

Dark clouds hovered and lightning struck
over a villa in Tuscany, where
a pompous heir lay in bed.

Afraid to go into the dark, he rambled on,
pleaded with the heavens,
for another year.

The earth trembled, the dark sky roared,
a gray bearded face appeared,
a distant voice whispered,

Son, you have squandered all your years,
hobnobbed with the rich, indulged
in women and wine,

Stolen from the weak, scorned the poor;
blinded by wealth and power,
you have lost your way.

Garden Of Life

You ask not for mercy, but another year?
A year cannot erase all your
wanton days.

The heir implored he would make amends,
go to church on Sundays,
do penance.

He swore to give up women and wine,
donate his money and time;
to no avail.

He lay there gazing in the distance,
soon the color left his face,
his voice faded.

The man in the clouds disappeared,
the heir breathed his last,
the curtain fell.

Seven Year Itch

Why are you staring at me like that?
It's not like my nose is growing long,
It's not like I have big Martian ears,
It's not like my teeth have fallen out.

Why are you staring at me like that?
It's not like I told on you to someone,
It's not like I took your precious wallet,
It's not like I ate your favorite cookies.

Why are you staring at me like that?
It's not like I've spent all your money,
It's not like I asked why you were late,
Or why you have lipstick on your face.

Why are you staring at me like that?
Because I love another, he let spill.
She threw china on the floor, crying:
After I paid for your law school fees?

They cussed, went to separate rooms,
She took her belongings and the kids,
Drove to her family home in Seattle,
After seven years, the two parted.

Journey

As teenagers, they spent hours talking on the phone,
Married after college, honeymoon in southern zone:
Music city Nashville, Smoky Mountains in Tennessee,
At Mardi Gras parade, cheered a float named Dixie.

Thirty years later, he had been diagnosed with cancer,
With memory loss, staggering walk, he felt like a loser.
Chemotherapy was debilitating, it got him nauseated,
He lost his hair, wore a cap and became so frustrated.

At the first blush of dawn, she woke up, made coffee,
Slumped in a chair, fueled herself with a big brownie.
Morning fog had not yet lifted, as she got him ready,
Buckled him in his seat, drove him for chemotherapy.

She enrolled him in a cancer-healing retreat program:
Spiritual camp – no chemotherapy, MRI or cardiogram.
Week of pampering massages, dose of psychotherapy,
Yoga, meditation, nature walks, dabbling with poetry.

Books and music were his escape, in his hour of quiet,
Immune-boosting vegan foods, daily therapeutic diet.
To lift his spirits, she joined him in yoga, meditation.
Two years later, doctor said, cancer was in remission.

Narcissist

He flaunts his swanky red Euro sports car,
walks into the room with a bit of swagger,
brags about his trips and stock portfolio;

wears a faux smile and the finest silk ties,
dines at fancy places with pretty women,
but his love affairs often end up in tatters;

he has an insatiable appetite for control,
blames everyone when he falls in trouble,
but cronies feed his ego, sing his praises;

he steps on toes scaling corporate ladder,
trusts no one save his old golden retriever,
who returns his love and never questions;

his father's passing was a rude awakening,
a silly quarrel had kept the two men apart,
the love he long sought, now lost forever;

therapy sessions helped him cope with loss,
shed old habits, buckle down and work hard,
a changed man he was after introspection.

Puffs

He walked his terrier, took out the garbage,
helped his wife and gladly did the dishes,
even volunteered time at the soup kitchen.

She bought housewares from a thrift store,
clothing from a nearby consignment shop,
saved money for the church donation box.

They were a hardworking, jolly old couple,
joined neighbors for barbeques and picnics,
vacationed when there was money to spare.

He had been smoking since he was sixteen,
now at sixty-one, his lungs were so hurting,
at times he broke into long coughing spells.

Hard as he tried, he could not quit smoking,
so his wife decided to keep him company;
each time he lit a cigarette, she also lit one.

It troubled him so to see her huff and puff;
as weeks rolled by, he lit fewer cigarettes,
one day he went cold turkey, it pleased her.

A Rewarding Life

Tom, a young lawyer, in the southern state of Virginia, represented a black man in court, whose ancestral land was being seized by eminent domain, for a mere song.

Jerome's ancestors were brought as slaves to America, on a cargo ship from Africa — it reminded Tom of his grandparents, who once owned slaves on a plantation.

Jerome won the court case, got to keep his property, told Tom of his yearlong visit to the land of his roots, felt blessed he had lent a hand to the less privileged.

Tom mulled over his life, he had traveled far and wide; despite his successful law career, he felt a lurking void, so he took a sabbatical to find himself and truth in life.

Garden Of Life

To West Africa he set sail, land of the former slaves,
touched by poverty, hunger, diseases, child labor and
poor sanitation, extended his stay to help bring change.

He met with village leaders to discuss rural solutions,
reached out to family, friends, Doctors-Without-Borders,
with aid, villagers drank clean water, diseases tempered.

Village to village he went and worked with non-profits
for change: built homes, brought water and solar energy,
got children off farms and mines, and into the schools.

Tom found helping rural folks a rewarding experience,
his past life of luxury and sports cars melted before him,
he stayed back in West Africa to help the less fortunate.

Garden Of Life

The Salt March

Train accidents are common in India, each year so many die;
mother of a four-year-old girl died in one such tragic incident.

Father lost a leg, was on crutches, could not care for his girl,
a live-in maid cooked and cleaned and ran errands for them.

One day, he visited an orphanage, there met with the owner,
after the meeting, a relative gave him a ride home in his car.

On the way, they stopped at a cafeteria, chatted over lunch;
the relative—a professor—asked what had brought him to town.

Looking for a new home for my girl, as I can't do much for her;
professor and wife had no children, he offered to raise the girl.

I cannot ask you for such a big favor, widower said with a sigh,
Don't worry, we'll raise her as our own, said the kind professor.

Few days later, professor and wife stopped by, picked up the
little girl from her home, they saw her as a gift from the Gods.

Widower realized he could not find anyone better to raise Anju,
the couple had an impeccable reputation and were well settled.

He accompanied his little girl, put her at ease in her new home,
gave his cousin a woolen wrap, to his wife a silk sari and sweets.

Garden Of Life

When he bid goodbye, little Anju held on to his hand and wept.
Smile dear, you look so pretty when you smile. I'll see you soon.

Few days later, she called her father with news that thrilled him:
Papa, Uncle got me nice puppy. I call him Yogi. You'll like him.

He saw his daughter once a month, told her stories of Gandhi,
took a trip to Gandhi Ashram, on the banks of River Sabarmati.

They walked the halls of what was once Gandhi's humble home,
in a corner sat a charkha, where he often spun yarn from cotton.

On the grounds stood few chalets and a large open prayer area,
where people chanted songs, read from Gita, Bible, and Quran.

It was from here that Gandhi led the famous 1930 Dandi March,
hundreds walked to the Arabian Sea, to protest Britain's salt tax.

Picking a fistful of salt from the shore, he urged Indians to make
their own salt—the British arrested him and 60,000 for defiance.

Anju graduated from a medical college, at the top of her class,
months later, Papa passed, she wept, and was brokenhearted.

She visited Gandhi ashram, this time with her adopted parents,
brought fond memories of her Papa and their monthly outings.

The First Buddha
Siddhartha Gautama Buddha

At the Himalaya foothills in Kapilavastu, by the gardens of Lumbini,
lived King Shuddhodana Gautama of the Shakya dynasty,
where flowed pristine River Rohini.

Twenty years after the king wed Maya, a son's birth brought a glow,
alas, days later, the queen departed for heavenly abode,
then joy soon gave way to woe.

If the prince stays at the palace, he will be a ruler or military leader,
said a hermit to the king, but if he wants to be a preacher,
he will become a spiritual teacher.

The king groomed his son for the throne, he had a princely aura,
he was wed in his teens to the lovely Princess Yashodhara,
while sweet music played on a sitara.

The prince one day ventured out, saw the ill and old lying curled,
met a monk, asked him why he had renounced the world,
how had he as a free man unfurled?

Siddhartha reflected on his lavish life, it no longer felt so right,
even birth of his son had not brought him much delight;
he reflected on it, night after night.

He shaved his head, renounced all he had, in a robe left home,
rested at a retreat by a stream, amid places unknown;
in search of truth, he did roam.

Garden Of Life

In Varanasi, five monks joined him in his *Dharma* truth mission,
they taught him discipline and deep meditation,
and to fast unto starvation.

When the prince accepted cup of rice from a village girl unknown,
the monks abandoned him, said he must atone,
so the prince traveled alone.

For six years he had lived an ascetic life, and not found Nirvana,
having wandered far from home in the Himalaya,
he now arrived at Bodh Gaya.

One full moon night, while he meditated under a Bodhi tree,
Mara, the devil, lured him with his daughters three;
prince fell not for his crafty plea.

In search of truth, he sat under the tree, senses heightened,
one day he conquered his demons, then awakened
as Buddha Shakyamuni, the enlightened.

Seeds of wisdom soon sprang from River Ganges to Yangtze,
a few heart-shaped leaves fell off the sacred tree,
and found their way into history.

Lord Brahma asked Buddha to preach *Dharma*, so the sanyasi
rejoined the five monks he had met in Varanasi,
known as Lord Shiva's city of Kashi.

Garden Of Life

Life is full of suffering, said Buddha, world is constantly changing,
free yourself from attachments and craving,
and you will find Nirvana waiting.

The Bodhisattva preached noble truths to unravel life's mystery:
curb your desires to end grief of life's journey,
meditate, free yourself from misery.

Forty-five years he taught the eight-fold path: to shun hate, fear,
temptation, aggression, greed, ego, hope and anger;
until one day he fell ill in Kushinagar.

Man's mind may turn him into beast or Buddha, said the beacon,
enslaved by world trappings, he becomes a demon,
enlightened, he finds truth and freedom.

Do not taint your soul with lies or steal things from your brothers,
do not kill a living thing or speak callously of others,
seek simplicity in life, do not ruffle feathers.

Rise like a white lotus flower, be calm, be humble, be pure of mind,
rise above the murky waters, be supple like vine,
rise, bloom like a full moon and sunshine.

At eighty, Buddha attained Nirvana, his ashes strewn amid flowers,
across ten nations, in the serenity of holy towers,
where he once sought refuge in their bowers.

Garden Of Life

His last words to disciples: Behold O monks, all elementary things
in the world are changeable, they are not lasting;
work toward salvation, for it is everlasting.

His Dharma Wheel orbits today, with four noble truths and liberating
eight-fold path to Nirvana, freedom from unrelenting
karmic cycle of reincarnation and suffering.

Some say Buddha chose his time, place, caste and royal relations,
to prove noble breed cannot escape life's tribulations,
or be assured of a ticket to salvation.

On a Full Moon day in May, Buddha's life and death we celebrate,
snuff out ignorance and hate, pray for hostilities to abate,
for peace and enlightenment we lie in wait.

Born in Lumbini, raised in Kapilavastu was Gautama Buddha,
enlightened in Bodh Gaya, spread Dharma in Isipatana;
in Kushinagar, he attained Pari-Nirvana.

Garden Of Life

Never Too Old To Dream

When we are young, we embrace our fantasies,
sometimes dreams dissipate with harsh realities,
until new doors open with the blooms of Spring,
lift our spirits, prime us for what life may bring.

We crest another hill, overcome our trivial fears,
challenge inner critics, journey to distant spheres,
dauntless of hurdles, never retreating to a corner,
we sprint forward with new confidence and vigor.

With age, we realize our careers have plateaued,
accept our limitations, decipher life's new code,
find pluck and passion to embrace new dreams,
wonder if we can achieve them within our means.

Travel, volunteering, reading, writing, painting,
I wound up living my dream – reading, writing;
sometimes I wondered, if time was on my side,
if the book would publish before came the tide.

War & Peace

Garden Of Life

Woodstock & War

For three days they came, hippies and all to Bethel,
indulged in booze, drugs, sex at the music festival,
they sang and danced merrily, in rain and in shine,
while our brave ones dodged bullets far in Vietnam.

Men, women in faded jeans, long hair, gathered at
parks to hear peace songs, some with shaven heads,
saffron clothing, chanted Haré Rama, Haré Krishna,
as U.S. dropped Agent Orange in jungles of Vietnam.

Anti-Vietnam war protestors took to the city streets
on Fifth Avenue, by the New York City Public Library,
peddlers sold war souvenirs — *Make Love Not War*,
love and peace buttons to passers-by on the street.

It was 1969, Americans had just landed on the moon,
city folks celebrated Mets beat the Baltimore Orioles,
women, civil rights and peace activists marched, while
our war heroes came home — the armless, the legless.

Garden Of Life

A man in a poster in blue-and-white striped pants,
with a red bowtie and star-spangled white top hat,
beckoned all passers-by... *Uncle Sam Wants You*,
some fallen returned, burned beyond recognition.

Draft introduced, new troops soon recruited for war,
the rich and the poor enlisted for the same battles,
among them sons of politician, teacher and worker;
some dodged the draft and artfully fled to Canada.

Hemlines were short, stock market fared well during
the relentless war, until a treaty declared war's end;
yellow ribbon-decked trees welcomed our troops,
sadly, many did not return to green grass at home.

The same month, the U.S. stock market also crashed,
and the war-driven economy also took a nasty dive;
took two long years to recover from the recession,
but how does one mend when a loved one is gone?

Garden Of Life

The Great American Tragedy

One beautiful September morning of the new millennium,
the Hudson River flowed leisurely in a summer's delirium;
all at once, two jets crashed into the mighty Twin Towers,
buckled and burned them with gruesome lethal power.

Flames thrashed, smoke billowed, so it has been written,
ill winds blew, grit and ash flew, as bells tolled in Heaven;
icons of steel and glass, how they trembled and tumbled,
what took seven years to build, had in an hour crumbled.

Lo and behold, all at once a giant cloud of white soot rose,
chased people down city alleys, with such tsunami force;
ashes mingled with warm ashes, while all our hearts bled,
for the three thousand the sun had taken too soon to bed.

Calls to New York City went unanswered… all lines busy,
the Rector Street train station, also went down in the city,
for those who left empty chairs, we sing a song of peace,
for them we shall make music, and plant flowering trees.

The night before, as I recall, I saw a fine New York skyline,
the moon hung high, the river twinkled like sparkling wine;
a night later the city went dark, the world was in mourning,
Man in the Moon did not smile, river too stopped flowing.

Garden Of Life

While embers still burned, I visited the smoldering scene,
shattered into smithereens, lay remains of litany of dreams;
there in a mound of rubble, cracked glass and twisted steel,
lay ashes strewn of loved ones, silenced by destiny's wheel.

Amid the Hudson waters stood Lady Liberty, proud and tall,
holding high with grace, the freedom torch for one and all;
I wondered of the last moments, last emotions of the fallen,
last words of loved ones, who joined the Milky Way on 9/11.

Hunt began for Osama bin Laden in caves of Afghanistan,
NATO allies joined U.S. forces to bomb the land of Taliban,
airstrikes at Tora Bora, Jalalabad, Kandahar, and Kunduz,
with Kabul under siege, the Taliban fled like the mongoose.

One day, I visited firehouse Engine 54, Ladder 4 in midtown,
that lost a crew of fifteen at the grim rescue scene downtown;
anthrax scare, sirens wailing, military vehicles on the roads,
emotions in the city ebbed and flowed with FBI alert codes.

That November, we were blessed with Leonid meteor showers,
stardust sprinkled over Ground Zero, then it was raining stars;
my eyes feasted on the star-spangled pageant of that morning,
stars with tails, others with fine trails, falling, blessing, healing.

Garden Of Life

Ravages of War

I held my breath as ominous clouds swept over Baghdad,
Bradley tanks raced through the desert sandstorm of Iraq;
hundred-eighty thousand U.S. marines in chemical suits,
boldly marched into port-town of Basra, then to Nasiriya.

Shock and awe bombs sent a shudder through my spine,
as squadrons of fighter jets zipped through the dark skies;
missiles struck, bunkers busted, cluster bombs exploded,
oil fields of Rumaila burned – death, devastation all over.

Basra, Baghdad, Tikrit and Mosul, like dominoes they fell,
Babylon, ancient city of Mesopotamia, now a total wreck;
cradle of civilization in ruins, Saddam's palaces leveled,
museums plundered, but no one did stop the bloody war.

Water and food lines in war-torn Basra, sad sight to watch,
bridges falling into Euphrates and Tigris rivers, so it was;
history rewritten with fall of Saddam's statue in Baghdad,
but euphoria short-lived, as Iraqis fled in despair to Syria.

My heart wept profusely as grisly scenes unfolded on TV,
prisoners of war at Abu Ghraib jail treated so inhumanely;
as battle raged in Fallujah, civil war loomed in the country,
fire crackled in the air, river of blood flowed through cities.

Garden Of Life

USS Abraham Lincoln hailed *Mission Accomplished* flag,
as President George Bush declared major combat's end;
twenty years after Desert Storm, a dictator's regime fell,
band played a victory song, still the brutal battle wore on.

Alas, Baghdad's Mutanabbi Street rocked by car bomb,
a bookstore-lined street, the soul of literary community;
where scholars, journalists, poets gathered at tea stalls,
smoked water pipes and debated the grim state of war.

As for weapons of mass destruction, cleanup after war
unearthed some fifty thousand abandoned rusty shells;
shells used by Iraq army during 1980 invasion of Iran,
American troops exposed to this lethal mustard agent.

Scores dead, brother killed brother: Shiite, Sunni, Kurd,
U.S. hanged Saddam Hussein, his sons too were slain;
as flag-draped coffins brought home our fallen braves,
many asked: Were the spoils of war and oil worth it?

Void left by U.S. exit was soon filled by ISIS militants,
who spread terror in the Arab lands – of Iraq and Syria;
while American troops came home from a long war to
a nation entrenched in deep recession and pessimism.

Papa, Make Bad War Go Away

A little boy in tears said to his father,
Papa, there is no milk at home to drink.
    When the curfew is lifted, I'll get some milk,
    father replied, hugging his five-year old son.
Papa, big brother hurting from gunshot,
Make his pain go away, so we can play.
    If I could make his pain go away, I would.
    Let us pray the war in Syria ends soon, son.
Papa, I want to eat Shish Barak today,
Mama says, there is no meat at home.
    When the soldiers go home, I will get meat,
    I'll ask Mama to make you Baba Ghanoush.
Papa, why no lights in our house?
Mama burn candles, I like candles.
    Bad people waiting outside our home, son.
    We don't want them to know we live here.
Papa, make bad war go away, I get scared,
I cannot sleep when it Boom, Boom outside.
    If I could make bad war go away, I would,
    If I could make us happy again, I would.

Don't Cry Wolf

How many banners will you wave, to declare another combat;
how many protests will it take, to stop
the drumbeats of war?

How many lies must we be told, to justify yet another battle;
how many people must die, before
the river runs red?

How many bombs will be blown, before hearts are numbed;
how many bullets does it take, to bury
a man's head in sand?

There are times when we must rise to defend our country,
or when genocide is carried out,
against humanity.

You who love to play war games, send others to frontline,
you who seek to profit from war,
have to answer to God.

Bury Your Weapons

Alexander, Napoleon, and Genghis Khan,
all went to war at the sound of a bugle call;
they rode their own steed, fought gallantly,
alongside their knights, they too sacrificed.

with shields, swords, on stallions they rode;
today the chief does not ride with his forces,
he can send missiles and unmanned drones,
drop nuclear bombs, wipe out entire towns.

leaps in technology help men to play God,
kill or clone humans, even sheep in a lab;
perform sex change or create deadly virus,
alas, fear and respect for the Lord is lost.

if God wishes to lighten the load on earth,
he would beam us up at his own free will;
so bury your bombs, missiles and drones,
arm yourselves with love, peace on earth.

Garden Of Life

Enemy Within

In the new millennium, globalism fever,
Drove U.S. companies to pull the outsourcing lever,
They laid off workers, watched their companies' stocks soar,
Cost-cutting acts rewarded the shareholders, most of all the CEO.

Corporate America sent factory jobs to China,
Sold genetically modified seeds from Africa to Asia,
These seeds require toxic chemical pesticides and fertilizers,
GMO seeds pollute the fields, cause infertility and deadly cancers.

Then came the roaring Great Recession,
Big banks were bailed, income gap saw explosion,
A few at the top received lavish perks and sterling benefits,
American dreams shattered, but multinationals reaped big profits.

Still, I have high hopes for America's vision,
Land of vast opportunities and incredible innovation,
If only the media would remember their pact to the people,
Not quash stories or be deceitful, but fly with honor like an eagle.

Time to rebuild America, not appease socialists,
Time to reign in runaway globalism, corporate lobbyists,
Time to care for veterans who serve nation with brave deeds,
Time to mend our torn tapestry with red-white-and-blue beads.

Garden Of Life

Eye For An Eye

An eye for an eye,
leaves the whole world blind.
    – Mahatma Gandhi

Where are the brave,
with noble hearts,
the unsung heroes,
who march to the drum of
the humanitarian call?
Send in the torchbearers,
sages and peacemakers,
catalysts of change,
champions of causes;
beckon them to stop these wars,
before they destroy us all;
summon the visionaries,
mavericks and trailblazers,
vanguards and pioneers,
leaders and thinkers,
rocks of Gibraltar,
masters of ceremony;
bid them all to light the torch,
be our beacon of hope,
for new horizons;
in a war, there are no winners,
only losers;
this hi-tech prowess,
these machine guns,

Garden Of Life

these cluster bombs,
this mighty show of arms,
these missiles, these drones,
these weapons of mass destruction,
aimed to maim or kill,
show our regress as humans.
rich nations defend themselves
against missiles and rockets,
with Iron Domes;
poor nations have no such
defense mechanisms;
they are decimated,
by hi-tech military weapons;
you who kill in the name of Islam,
for the love of Allah,
lay down your arms;
be a Gandhi, not a jihadi,
pursue peace like Buddha,
honor women and children,
break bread with your brethren;
and you, arms dealers,
who profit from selling weapons,
to rogue countries and criminals—
why you have sold your soul for money?

Garden Of Life

Stain on American Tapestry

Slave trade Bills of Sale at the Atlanta History Center:
Hariet sold in 1860 for $1,150, Lucy in 1861 for $600,
Thomas and Naun, sold as a pair in 1863 for $2,500,
Woven into Black History in America's deep south.

A year later, Atlanta sieged, Civil War ended slavery.
Abe's Union Party won the war, Confederates ceded;
but blacks were stilled lynched by the Ku Klux Klan,
woven into Black History in America's deep south.

As Atlanta rose from its ashes, Henry Grady's vision
of an industrial New South, aimed to eventually erase
the deep divide between the blacks and the whites –
separate schools, restrooms that made Black History.

Jim Crow's segregation laws, white-hooded figures
of Ku Klux Klan members on horses, KKK pamphlets,
showcased at Atlanta History Center year after year;
woven into Black History in America's deep south.

Garden Of Life

Rosa Parks' refusal to give her bus seat to white man
led to civil rights crusade, a 1965 voting rights march
led by Martin Luther King from Selma to Montgomery,
woven into '60s Black History in America's deep south.

2016: White supremacist youth fatally shot nine blacks
at a South Carolina church, opening deep old wounds;
along came Bree Newsome who climbed the flagpole,
took down Confederate flag at the Statehouse grounds.

Newsome handcuffed, taken into custody amid cheers,
as white and black activists protested all across town;
the Confederate flag, seen as a slavery icon by Blacks,
now a relic at the Military Museum near the Statehouse.

King's *I Have a Dream* speech called for sons of slaves
and sons of former slaveowners to cut bread together;
the sun may have set in 1865 for slavery in the south,
but a new civil war lingers in 2020, sparked by politics.

A New Tomorrow

Still stunned by the enemy within,
remorse over the road not taken?

our yesterdays and today are gone,
but what about our new tomorrows?

light a torch to illuminate our path,
a path that will lead to renaissance.

ill winds are still bearing down on us,
come, what are we all waiting for?

time to reflect on our past missteps,
time to find strength in our hearts,

wounds still healing, scars remind
we have braved the mighty storms,

we have emerged from deep dark,
we had been at war with each other,

we shall carve out a new tomorrow.
come, what are we waiting for?

Garden Of Life

XXXXXXXXXXXXXXXXXXXXXXXXXXXXXXXXXXXXXX
XXXXXXXXXXXXXXXXXXXXXXXXXXXXXXXXXXXXXX
XXX   ***   XXX
XXX   ***   XXX
***

Rise America, Rise

Rise America Rise, time for us to shine.

To your future I toast with my glass of wine.

Tomorrow is a new day, build a new enterprise.

Rise, keep old friends, make new allies at sunrise.

Protect nation from scandal, enemy, and conspiracy.

Soar like the bald eagle, light the torch of Lady Liberty.

Fight injustice and poverty, restore nation to our old glory.

A country once hailed for its vision, innovation and technology.

Ring Liberty Bell, ring, ring, ring, splendid horizon is within our sight.

Rise America Rise, with our tenacity we can boldly scale to new height.

***

***

Live Life

May there be light in your life,
to chase away the fog and darkness;

May there be wind in your sails,
to take you to your next destination;

May you be blessed with wisdom,
have foresight to tell foe from friend;

May you have music in your life,
stay young at heart, forever curious;

May you live a long, happy life,
fly high with grace, dare and courage;

Be brave. Be bold. Be dauntless,
have faith… climb another mountain;

Be like the trees, always bending
with the wind, yet forever standing tall;

Life is what you want it to be,
may yours be filled with joy and blessings.

Red, White & The Blues

A Soldier's Story

VA Hospital doctor said I suffered from
an acute Post Traumatic Stress Disorder,
he advised me to go for weekly therapy;
our German Shepherd accompanies me.

My family has been my pillar of strength,
father, proud war veteran, cheers me up,
mother spoils me with my favorite meals,
my little brother, he runs errands for me.

Good God, I have seen it all: bombings,
airstrikes, bullets raining down on towns,
the maimed, the dead, broken families,
Why all this hate and wars in the world?

When our armored tank hit a land mine,
both my legs were blown up, then again
I was far luckier than some of my friends,
sadly, the music forever died for them.

I struggle to leave dark shadows behind,
blaring sirens, people rushing for cover,
demolished buildings, billowing smoke,
charred bodies, bloody streets, despair.

Garden Of Life

Here I sit in my shrink's big black chair,
remembering friends from my platoon,
who braved street battles alongside me,
dodged barrage of bullets from enemy.

Now at the VA physical therapy center,
in my prosthetic legs, spirits dampened,
I think to myself: If only I could have my
two legs back, I could climb Mt. Everest.

Another day, I go for a walk with my dog,
we stop at a stream, he goes for a drink,
then we sit at a bench, eat our sandwich,
I play the harmonica and he yodels along.

I once had a girl, we were so much in love,
then to Iraq I was sent, she said she'd wait,
wrote no more to her, when I lost my legs,
probably married by now, I miss her much.

There are times I have thought of taking
my life, then I am woefully reminded of
friends, whose lives were stolen too soon
from them. . . so I live on to honor them.

Garden Of Life

Love & Soup Kitchen

She worked as a clerk at the store,
came home, did household chores;
during recession, store shut down,
she looked for work in every town;

knocked on many doors for a job,
when car broke down, she did sob,
then she took the bus everywhere,
as she could not afford the repair;

husband worked at a local factory,
moonlighted for a bit extra money,
barely made enough to scrape by,
lunch was ham and cheese on rye;

then one day, all hell broke loose,
he came home, gulped some juice,
spilled the grim news with a frown,
Honey, my factory is closing down;

life was soup kitchen, food stamps,
thrift shops, coupons and oil lamps,
six years gone past, yet no offspring,
one day, he was huffing and puffing;

Garden Of Life

jobs scarce, purse strings stretched,
a year later, their home repossessed;
they moved in with her old mother,
then learned he had lung cancer;

no jobs, no funny stories to share,
besides church, ventured nowhere,
she baked quiches and apple tarts,
for bakeries and local food marts;

hospital visits for chemotherapy,
left him so exhausted and grumpy,
recovery came at slow steady pace,
brought tad color to his sallow face;

he took on odd jobs as a handyman,
did all he could do as a proud man,
to his wife, a vacation he pledged,
one morning, he lay cold in his bed.

Great Recession left lasting scars,
the rich fared well under the stars;
oligarchy is still the favorite game,
played by big boys without shame.

Garden Of Life

Hungry in New York City
Part 1

It happened long ago one afternoon,
at the Port Authority bus concourse,
a middle-aged man with a stubble,
in an old winter coat, ragged pants,
prematurely bent, carrying a knapsack,
walked over to a garbage receptacle,
muttering to himself.

He rummaged through the trash,
stumbled upon half a bagel,
brushed it and took a bite,
while I watched, tongue-tied;
here I was in the world's richest city,
there in front of me was a grown man,
looking for morsels in a trash can.

I approached the big man,
asked if he was hungry;
he gave me a sheepish nod;
we walked into a hamburger joint.
Sir, how about a hamburger and shake?
Vanilla shake, please ma'am.
Minutes later, I walked to the table,
carrying a shake and paper bag,
with hamburger and fries.
Thanks lady, he said, then took a bite.
Enjoy your lunch, I said and left.

Garden Of Life

Part II

Yesterday, city had multi-millionaires,
greed and corruption at every bend,
politicians bought by highest bidder,
today, many New Yorkers have fled.

isn't it time to stop and ask ourselves:
how the wealthy came into such riches,
how many toes have they stepped on,
how many have they bilked or bribed?

public schools been closed for a year,
why should socialist politicians care,
their children attend private schools,
COVID did not disturb their schedule.

it reminds me of the three monkeys,
who shut their mouths, eyes, and ears,
to all the hunger, poverty, and crime,
and politicians with ill-gotten money.

Garden Of Life

A Ray of Sunshine

His name, Ray, as a ray of sunshine,
works on New York City's east side;
clad in blue jeans, gray fleece cap,
he makes a living doing odd tasks.

He has no luck with a steady job,
when employers learn he lives at
the homeless shelter in Brooklyn,
they callously say: Position Filled.

That makes him feel awfully sad,
but he shows no woe on his face,
greets everyone with sunny smile,
seldom sings the blues or whines.

Hard times Ray had seen plenty,
father walked out on the family,
mother died when he was a teen,
but he hums along a happy song.

Garden Of Life

When days are long, tempers short,
many like him end up on skid row;
not Ray, he is a perpetual optimist,
with faith and belief in humanity.

With his kind mild-mannered ways,
people gladly give him few chores,
as well as food and warm clothes;
such kind gestures uplift his spirits.

One winter morning, a young lady
invited him to a nearby donut shop,
got him a donut and hot chocolate,
gave him a twenty-dollar gift card.

Next week, when she ran into him,
he shared the good news of his job:
stocking groceries on store shelves;
just in time for a Merry Christmas.

Living High on Wall Street

Ah, the lives of well-heeled Wall Street brokers,
with skeletons in their closets, cocaine in pockets,
bankers and brokers who own yachts and planes,
some like Bernie Madoff, played Ponzi games.

Bartenders at a Wall Street restaurant once sold
white powder to Street addicts in folded napkins,
a bank's chief kept cocaine in an antacid bottle,
a broker, who dispensed it at work, imprisoned.

Illegal drugs for cash, favors, stock information,
indulged even by Street's hedge fund managers,
such decadent lifestyle and risky insider trading,
have dragged Street brokers, executives to jail.

The unscrupulous CEOs and Wall Street bankers,
have much influence in the corridors of Congress,
they send lobbyists and lawyers to Capitol Hill,
sway nation's policies made by elected officials.

Garden Of Life

The Gambler

Stock market goes up,
it goes down, the gambler's
mood sways all week with the market;

poor Mr. Gambler,
like a small-time investor,
hoping to strike it rich, he took risks.

like a lucky beginner,
he was a happy instant winner,
bought a new home, reinvested gains;

got an adrenaline rush,
trading in high-flying stocks,
then plunged into commodity options;

read coffee and oil charts,
bet crude oil prices would decline,
alas, they shot up all through the night;

he became so irate,
could not even think straight,
blamed the world for all his mistakes.

now, knee-deep in debt,
he lost his home and his family,
friendly tip turned out to be a scam.

On Death Row

It was the day of his execution;
his lawyer's appeals for a lighter sentence —
life imprisonment,
had been denied.
Garcia, a car salesman,
father of two,
who had migrated at five to America
with his family from Mexico,
spent his last days
at the Allan B. Polunsky Unit jail,
a concrete whitewashed structure
in West Livingston, Texas,
the last abode for
death-row inmates.

A shadow lurked in Garcia's cell,
chuckles shattered the silence;
it irked him,
he scanned the room;
nobody there.
Satan was there.

As he awaited news
of the governor's pardon,
he was haunted by his neighbor,
who threw wild cocaine parties;
one Friday night, music blared,
the rowdiness next door,
kept his children up.

Garden Of Life

Garcia went next door,
asked the neighbor to tone it down,
but he cussed him instead,
and slammed the door.

Next morning, when Garcia
stepped out with his dog,
to fetch the newspaper,
the neighbor drove by,
fired rapid shots from his car,
then sped away;
next moment, the dog lay bleeding
on the driveway.
Garcia was heartbroken,
the dog had been family for years,
he wondered if the shot was meant for him;
later that day, he banged
on the neighbor's door,
shot him in cold blood.

He recalled a distant day when he was
booked at the county jail,
clean-shaven, a crew-cut,
the humbling strip-search,
pair of sneakers, white shirt, and pants,
he was given to wear;
it was a searing summer day,
no air conditioning in prison cells,
hallways reeked of putrid air,

Garden Of Life

inmates watched as he was led,
and confined to his cell;
no privacy in jail.

He exercised in the prison yard,
did not mingle with inmates
in the dining hall,
talked to his family,
on the jail-monitored telephone,
occasionally got a book
from the prison cart,
now and then, a tap on his shoulder,
made him turn around;
nobody there;
the evil force was there.

The early morning wake-up call
jerked him out of bed;
he washed up, went for breakfast,
at six o'clock reported for work;
some inmates cooked,
some did loads of laundry,
some cleaned, did maintenance,
a few assigned to light industrial labor;
for compensation, they received privileges
and a good conduct card.

Garcia reflected on his life —
he had been a good family man,

Garden Of Life

followed the rules of the road,
on weekends, coached soccer;
if only the neighbor had not shot his dog;
he recalled the moment the jury
had found him guilty of
first degree murder;
although shaken by the verdict,
he showed no remorse for
gunning down his neighbor.

He recounted his transfer in iron chains,
from the county jail
to the Polunsky Unit,
where he was photographed,
finger-printed, got a crewcut,
and was taunted by prison guards
during a strip-search;
fearing reprisal,
he stayed silent.

His lawyer had warned they would test him,
even try to break him;
as required by the prison,
he deloused with a lice-killer,
wore a white jumpsuit,
with initials "DR" Death Row,
in large black letters on the back,
then went for a medical checkup.
Satan was at his heels.

Garden Of Life

Garcia hated the Polunsky Unit,
the strip-search before every shower,
meals served through a slot in his cell door;
once, when he had chest pains,
he asked to see the doctor,
but his request was ignored;
he asked to see the warden,
but his request was denied;
enraged, he punched his cell wall,
until his knuckles bled;
solitary confinement
drove him out of his mind.

He thought of hanging himself in his cell,
but a ray of light streaming in
from the tiny window,
kept his hope alive
for the governor's pardon.

At times, he dreamt his neighbor was
chasing him, down the street in his car,
in the dark of the night;
he broke out in cold sweat;
jumped out of bed,
hyperventilating,
trembling, heart pounding;
he tried to dispel his fears,
confront his demons,
but life seemed to be slipping away,

Garden Of Life

as if a riptide was sweeping him out to sea;
tormented by deafening inner voices,
he wallowed in misery;
so he read the Bible before bedtime.
Satan then disappeared.

Then came the Swan Song.
Garcia was lost in thoughts when
a prison guard entered his cell,
handcuffed and shackled him,
and hauled him away,
no word from the governor yet;
a three-vehicle convoy transported him
to the Huntsville Unit in Texas,
for his final hours and
execution.

Garcia felt a void inside,
like a wilted garden with no flowers,
a street with barren trees;
he yearned to be back home with family,
hug and kiss them,
cry out he loved them,
apologize for the sadness,
he had brought in their lives,
alas, it was too late.

After a cavity search, he was placed
in a holding cell, for his last meal.

Garden Of Life

but he had no appetite today,
no word from the governor yet;
a chaplain stopped by his cell,
read him a passage
from the Bible;
clad in white jumpsuit and
in chains, Garcia was led
to the execution chambers;
watching from the windows were
his wife, his brother and father,
victim's family members,
the executioner and his assistant,
Department of Corrections director,
the jail's chaplain, two doctors,
the county judge, the sheriff,
and members of the media.

Now at death's door,
Garcia did not show remorse or apologize
to the victim's family;
teary-eyed, his family watched
as he was strapped to the gurney,
and injected with a lethal solution;
soon the room spun around him,
slowly the color left his face,
seven minutes later,
Garcia was pronounced dead.
Satan laughed.
Jesus wept.

Stolen Childhood

Garden Of Life

Jaws of Hell

Born into a poor southern family who could ill-afford her care,
tossed from one foster home to another, Cecelia's nightmare;
many who sheltered her were hungry for a government check,
trafficked her, never worried her life was an emotional wreck.

No time to play, night after night, like a caged bird she wept,
sometimes abused by surrogates in whose care she was kept;
sold into sex slavery, at thirteen gave birth to a biracial son,
the identity of her child's father, sadly she would never learn.

The little girl's childhood was mercilessly stolen from her,
by man's thoughtless behavior for his momentary pleasure;
an angel heard her cries and freed her from the caged shell,
a foster couple took her home, away from fiery jaws of hell.

Cecelia loved her new parents, was tucked in bed with kisses,
she vacuumed, dusted home, gladly helped with the dishes;
loved her son dearly, sadly had to give him up for adoption,
now married, mother of two girls, gives them her attention.

Many like Cecelia have suffered far worse, contracted AIDS,
even died young, caught in a trap of cruel sex slave trades.

Garden Of Life

Flying Trapeze

She was floating, flying in a fancy costume on a trapeze,
she was bouncing, jumping, waving from a trampoline,
she was dancing and prancing and went into a rope spin,
she was swinging high till the red-nosed clowns came in.

All the world loves a circus and the daring trapeze artist;
this pretty one was abducted from Nepal by a con artist,
who saw her walk home alone from school one fine day,
asked a question, pushed her in his car and drove away.

Traded to an agent and sold in India to a circus manager,
who ruthlessly beat her, to his heart's content raped her;
her family might even think she had run away from home,
never knowing that she was snatched on her way home.

Every town she performed, children flocked to the circus,
had popcorn, cotton candy and then clapped in chorus;
she waved flying kisses to her fans, but a song in her heart
cried for freedom, as she swung high and played her part.

Many like the trapeze artist are victims of cruelty and rape,
they live sad lonely lives, but have no channels of escape.

Garden Of Life

Escape From Fate

Snatched at twelve, her mama's baby,
since then passed from man to man,
seven days a week, abused by them,
never caring if she hurt or even bled,
her faith in God kept her spirits high;

this morning, as she caresses her pain,
looks outside her blue latticed window,
sees the clouds drifting, birds chirping,
wonders if she can from her cage flee,
lets the wings of her dreams soar free;

free from the wicked world caving in,
free from the clutches of suppression,
free from the crude hands of invaders,
free from her monstrous manipulators,
free from the chains of soul enslavers;

one misty night she pulls off a plot,
slits her blue six-yard sari into three,
knots all pieces into one long piece,
drops it from the bathroom window,
slides her petite frame through it;

Garden Of Life

sari dangles high above the ground,
she jumps off on the soft green turf,
runs fast before mean madam hears,
of her clandestine escape in the dark,
and sends the goons in pursuit of her;

she paces fast in the pre-dawn hours,
melts into the shadows as men pass,
comes upon a temple, makes a stop,
goes to the rear, there rests on a cot,
drifts off into the dark of the night;

fog lifts over the hills the next morn,
the tweetle-dee birdies wake her up,
temple guardian finds her on the cot,
brings a porridge bowl for breakfast,
pulls up a chair and lends her his ear;

She pleads him to rescue the others,
those held captive against their will;
police called, raid on ill repute house,
madam is now trapped like a mouse;
the young girl's family take her home.

Trail of Tears
Part I
Koidu Diamond Mines, Sierra Leone, W.Africa

Little boy, little boy, why are you crying?
Papa got beaten by big man at the mine.
Little boy, nice boy why was Papa there?
Papa work at the mine for long, long time.

Little boy, good boy, where is your Mama?
Mama gone to work in far away rice fields.
Little boy, brave boy, where do you live?
Me live in Kono, but I . . .I always hungry.

Little boy, sweet boy, do you go to school?
No school. Papa say to work at the mine.
Little boy, fine boy, what is your name?
KWABLA. Mama say I born on Tuesday.

Kwabla, why Papa and you work at the mine?
Big man with cane make Papa and me work.
Papa say there are shiny stones inside rock.
Big man sell shiny stones to the bad people.

Bad people give big man many guns to fight,
They all shout loud, ask for more shiny stones,
Big man get angry, he pull out his small gun,
Then he go Bang! Bang! I get scared. I hide.

Garden Of Life

Part II
Marange Diamond Fields, Zimbabwe, W.Africa

Little boy, little boy, why are you crying?
I tired. I work ten hours every day at mine.
Little boy, nice boy, where is mama, papa?
No Mama. No Papa. I slave boy. I'm eight.

Little boy, good boy, do you go to school?
No school. I work, go home, eat and sleep.
Little boy, sweet boy, do you have friends?
Many friends. Everyone say they like me.

Little boy, brave boy, where do you live?
In a bamboo hut with nine very big boys.
Little boy, fine boy, what is your name?
GAMBA. Big man there call me Soldier.

Gamba, what do you have in your pan?
Boy hums, sifts his sieve in muddy water.
Little Gamba, your fingers are bleeding.
No problem, my fingers always bleed.

His dark eyes gleam, he smiles, bares his
white teeth against his soft mocha skin.
Look! Look Mister! I found a lucky rock.
Big man with cane walks down to get it.

Blood Diamonds

Hear laughter of boys panning in the riverbeds.
Hear the cries of men lynched in mining camps.
Hear cane-wielding rebel lead badger workers.
Hear busy traders talk of smuggling diamonds.

These conflict diamonds of Sierra Leone, used
to fund the Revolutionary United Front rebels,
who fought the country's long civil war and
kidnapped young ones to work at the mines.

One million diamond diggers, scores of panners,
work in unsanitary and hazardous environments,
exploited by rebels, politicians, rogue regimes,
who loot their countries and keep the proceeds.

This blood money, passed from hand-to-hand,
these toxic chemicals released into Save River,
this insatiable appetite for diamonds has led to
greed, corruption, bribery in the diamond land.

Rampant human rights abuses at Marange fields:
dog mauling, sexual assaults and torture camps,
carried out at these mines by Zimbabwe police,
and scores of fields across the African continent.

Reflecting Pool

Garden Of Life
Curio Cabinet
Part I

When I was a young teen
feeling the blues, music was my warm refuge.
I shut myself in the bedroom,

put on my favorite tunes
on a turntable that sat atop the curio cabinet,
which flaunted fancy tea sets,

dinnerware, silverware, glassware,
prisms, exotic seashells, and a face with a pipe
chiseled on a pale coconut shell;

on the bottom shelf lay folded
red-tasseled silk, filigreed-plastic, rice paper fans,
ladies in kimonos painted on them.

I opened the glass door,
reached for the exquisite fans that my father
had brought home from

his business trip to Japan,
then I leisurely sat on the edge of the bed,
tossed my head back,

and fanned my cares away,
like the graceful bourgeois ladies in a parlor,
on a hot summer day.

Garden Of Life

Part II

On the bottom shelf
also lay my father's dark walnut English pipe,
which he once stuffed with

sweet-scented tobacco,
kindled and stirred the leaves, and puffed until
they turned to ashes;

mother often complained,
the white café curtains in the room got discolored,
and the house reeked of tobacco,

so, half-heartedly my father
switched to the local cigarette, and the walnut pipe
was returned to the cabinet;

after reading the morning paper,
he took a break, had tea, then lit a cigarette
with a silver butane lighter,

and blew smoke rings in the air.
How do you make those curly rings?
I asked my father.

Curly rings?
Ah! That's a secret my dear, he replied
with a puckish grin;

in his tender years, he forgot
his comfort pipe that had once given him
hours of pleasure.

Garden Of Life

Part III

The bottom shelf
of the cabinet also boasted my big brother's
athletic trophies;

this morning, I found
mother in the veranda, trading the trophies
with a woman peddler,

who had a basket of wares;
there she sat in a sari wrapped around her loins,
tipping the hand-scale,

trophies in one tray,
weights in the other, as she argued and bargained
with my mother.

I walked up to her, grabbed
the trophies and said: These are not for sale,
you can have my old frocks instead;

placing the glassware basket
on her head, the woman walked away upset,
mumbling to herself;

mother threw me a hard stare,
as I returned my brother's prized accolades
to the curio cabinet;

many full moons later,
when I returned from school, an empty shelf
stared back at me.

Garden Of Life

Goodness gracious,
the silver trophies were gone, only last week
I had polished them all;

but, who was I to judge
my mother's frugal ways, for she had to feed
a family of eight;

the glass jars filled with
homemade pickles and jams, now lined the top
of our mirrored-armoire.

Part IV

After several years
in America, when I visited my home in India,
I asked my big brother

about the glass cabinet.
It's no more, he said, shaking his head,
the wares got heavy for it,

one day, it all came
crashing down — dinnerware, glassware,
tea sets, seashells, and all.

In my tender years,
memories come flooding fast of trophies, smokepipe,
and red-tasseled fans.

Those Good Old Days

Those good old days when
I lived a simpler Spartan life,
wore hand-me-down clothes,
played with a few basic toys.

Those good old days when
I put together jigsaw puzzles;
rented from a local bookstore
my favorite Enid Blyton novel.

Those good old days when
I loved to frolic in pouring rain,
father helped with my studies,
mother sewed pretty dresses.

Those good old days when
I played hopscotch, skip-rope,
twirled a hula hoop, donned in
a flared dress over cancan skirt.

Those good old days when
I played music on the jukebox,
loved to rock-n-roll and foxtrot,
waltz, twist, and do the cha-cha.

Garden Of Life

Those good old days when
family made vanilla ice cream
in an oak barrel, took turns to
crank it while we told stories.

Those good old days when
we all splashed colors on Holi,
set off fireworks on Dussehra,
dressed in our best for Diwali.

I miss those days of yesterday,
though we had no refrigerator,
no oven, no car, no telephone,
and used a lobby pay-phone.

I miss those days of yesterday,
no air-conditioner, no problem,
ceiling fans spun in every room,
no lack of friends or food either.

I miss those days of yesterday,
laughter came easy to my heart,
songs found their way to my lips,
worries were tossed to the wind.

Garden Of Life

Ode to My Brother

Once we were a large family of eight in India,
one left for Africa, four of us left for America;
you stayed back, took care of Mom and Dad,
Dad departed, then only Mom and you left.

Alas, in her golden years Mom was bedridden,
shortly thereafter, you went down a steep hill;
life snatched you too soon from us at sixty-six,
how I cherish your last days we spent together.

We listened to old melodies, exchanged stories,
watched cricket matches on TV and reminisced;
you had taught me to dance, when I was young,
I was a shy girl, you had given me confidence.

Three times a week, you went for kidney dialysis,
two days, you saw a doctor for pain in your legs;
night after night, you coughed relentlessly in bed,
I gave you tablespoon of honey, so you could rest.

You smiled through your pain, did not complain,
upon my return to America, to Avalon you sailed.

Garden Of Life

The Roads I Traveled

Born by candlelight in India's civil war,
never dreamed I would travel this far;
goodbye my land of sages and spice,
hello America, my pleasant surprise.

With passing years, many miles I rode,
in search of the Yellow Brick Road,
saw rugged coastlines, hairpin bends,
tricky forks, and oh, some dead ends.

Through all my travels, far and wide,
I searched the alleys and countryside,
from New York City to Napa Valley,
in the Golden State on a green trolley.

Time and again, I took the high road,
but found myself at more crossroads;
what I gained as the years unfurled,
is pound of knowledge of this world.

Don't Let Life Pass You By

Wake up to the bubble of the percolator,
savor your coffee, read the morning paper;
then take a walk in your primrose glasses,
if it rains, slip on your old yellow galoshes.

If perchance the world gets under your skin,
you can always count on your kith and kin;
if on your journey you arrive at an impasse,
fear not, like all storms, this too shall pass.

Live every moment with dare and passion,
like a river rushing to meet the big ocean;
scale another mountain, sail another sea,
follow your dreams, whatever they be.

Garden Of Life

Pearls of Life

They bring sunshine and love tarts,
leave tender trails in our soft hearts,
for them we build castles of dreams,
thru' them appreciate what life means.

They shower us with hugs and kisses,
turn our worries into a basket of blisses,
weave their stories with a magic brush,
fill our lives with much music and mirth.

Then one morning we wake up and find,
young ones have left their nests behind,
they have gone to fend for themselves,
for they are no longer the size of elves.

Now caring for young ones of their own,
they look back at years that have flown,
share pearls of wisdom with offspring,
laugh with them, count their blessings.

Garden Of Life

Footprints in the Sand

Tonight I write without any breaks,
heart and soul, whatever it takes;
I remind myself I must stay strong,
stretch the day to make it last long,
voice war's atrocities on humanity,
the road to peace has been rickety.

the road to peace has been rickety,
but that must not shake our tenacity;
we paved the way, braved the storm,
hoping to see many a noble reform;
considering it on a scope and scale,
we took the road with hills and dale.

we took the road with hills and dale,
for greater good despite strong gale;
eight ounces yin, eight ounces yang:
pound of happiness, Taoist' yin-yang;
now take this journey hand-in-hand,
leave fresh footprints in silver sand.

Garden Of Life

leave fresh footprints in silver sand,
my fate, is in the palm of my hand;
if I persevere and do not lose sight,
I shall pen the poem by late tonight,
take stock of all that I have learned,
until the midnight musk oil is burned.

Until the midnight musk oil is burned,
I shall write, leave no stone unturned,
unwind with wine, cheese and bread,
before retiring my tired limbs to bed;
tomorrow, I shall celebrate and play,
savor this life before time slips away.

savor this life before time slips away,
I'll put on lively music, sing and sway,
then write a new story set elsewhere,
of worn-out shoes, dress threadbare,
saleswoman who goes door to door,
sells wares from a consignment store.

Field of Shamrocks

If life be a road with litany of hurdles
and jagged rocks, I shall hopscotch,
like a tropical beady-eyed green frog.

If life be a book of noble inspiration,
with formulas for love and peace and
chemistry, I would read unto eternity.

If life be a rainbow after a big storm,
lend me a brush and canvas to paint
a fine mural of my life's adventures.

If life be a river of celestial harmony,
let me hear Pan play music on a pipe,
and Apollo pluck on the golden lyre.

If life be a goblet of red Cabernet,
fill it to the brim my friend, so I can
revel in St. Patrick playing the fiddle.

If life be a rolling field of shamrocks,
I shall thank my shining stars for all
that I have in my home and my yard.

Garden Of Life

House of Light

The house of cards will surely fall,
and the gates of heaven will close,
to all those who lie, cheat and steal;

build your house with strong walls,
cement it with love and lots of grit,
so it can weather mammoth storms;

open your doors to the kind and wise,
shut them to those who love to fight,
beware of folks in sheep's clothing;

open your windows, smell the roses,
hear birds chirp sweetly in the trees,
let the spiritual light into your life;

open your heart to welcome friends,
share tidings and laughs with them,
treasure these cherished memories.

Love and hate are opposite sides of the same heart. You choose.

Our Beautiful World

Garden Of Life

Sunset at Goa Beach

Strolling down the Calungate Beach in Goa,
reminded me of Hawaii, so I cried out, Aloha!

sun worshippers bronzing, gave a hand wave,
swimmers rose high with each surging wave;

children built little sandcastles with mud pails,
youngsters flew colorful kites with long tails;

a shack with "Baywatch" sign stood at a bend,
green surfboards at a kiosk, leaning at one end;

tourists sipped tall cocktails at a funky shack,
in a corner, a lady with a hat read a paperback;

parasailers sailed past as I took in a sunset treat,
whispering waves, how they hummed so sweet;

Garden Of Life

shifting sand, gingerly tickled under my feet,
seductive waters, how they rushed up to greet;

in the distance, throwing a last crimson blush,
the sun slipped in the balmy waters in a hush;

all at once, a giant wave unfurled like a sheet,
charged toward me, knocked me off my feet;

leaving behind surf and footprints in the sand,
I stopped to hear music played by a live band;

with salt of the Arabian Sea still on my lips,
I took the path of roses and yellow orchids;

past tall emerald palms and red bougainvillea,
to a cottage fringed by a hedge, Song of India.

The Waves

The waves, the waves, take me to distant shores,
The waves, the waves, they bring me back home.

The wind, the wind, kicks up surf and emotions,
Blows through my hair and sprays mist in the air.

The surf, the surf, it spawns ripples in my heart,
Rushes to the shore and crashes against the rocks.

The tide, the tide, it washes ashore exotic shells,
Leaves a fancy one at my feet, I feel so blessed.

The birds, the birds, flocking home to their nests.
Surfers come ashore, as I watch a serene sunset.

The waves, the waves, they dance under the stars.
The sun has gone to bed, moon reigns until dawn.

Garden Of Life

Summer in The Adirondacks

Summer is a splendid time to escape to
Adirondacks Mountains in New York,
let the gentle uplifting breeze blow
through your hair as you cruise on
the paddle-wheeler steamboat,
cheer the feisty regatta racers
at the dazzling Lake George,
watch electrifying concerts
under the stars at a park,
take a chairlift for divine
view from a mountain top,
savor the rustic nature trails,
listen to wise whispers emanate
from the spirits of lofty mountains,
if you care for swift adrenaline rush,
buckle up and go for the bungee jump,
then take the long drive up to Montreal,
walk down cobblestone streets of Quebec,
enjoy the finest French cuisine and ambiance,
as we did, when the children were oh so young.

As The Seasons Turn

The whispering wind, the rustling tree leaves,
radiant reds and yellows of oak and elms,
fall off their limbs, cover the grounds.
Autumn is here.

The gusty wind blows away a man's toupée,
pine cones plummet from the evergreens,
they will adorn the Christmas tree.
Holiday spirit in the air.

The grounds are now swathed in soft white,
stockings hang for gifts from Santa,
children sledding down the hill.
Old man winter is here.

They throw snowballs and build a Snowman,
dress him in scarf, hat and red mittens,
give him a long carrot for his nose.
Days later, Frosty no more.

Rain pitter-patters on the trees and rooftops,
with lightning rods and the thunderclaps,
children read Curious George books.
Spring is in the air.

Garden Of Life

Yellow daffodils, pink tulips bring much cheer,
azaleas and rhododendrons are in bloom,
cherry blossoms in profusion.
Time to seed tomatoes.

Lawnmowers are roaring in the neighborhood,
children playing in the yards and pools,
barbeque grills are all fired up.
Glad summer is here.

They play Lego blocks, visit amusement parks,
rush to Good Humor truck for ice cream,
go figure skating at an indoor rink.
Almost back to school time.

They learn the ABCs from Sesame Street on TV,
bring books from the local library to read,
do homework, play with the new dog,
Carve pumpkin for Halloween.

Autumn is here, the leaves fall off the tree again,
dog runs through crunchy bronze leaves;
children grow up as the seasons turn,
Time flies, with no return.

God's Palette

I sit by a window lost in thoughts,
of the years that have gone past,
see autumn leaves cling to trees,
in hues of russet, red, and gold.

The leaves soon fall off the trees,
turn to copper, become crunchy,
the wind hustles in with a surge,
gathers the leaves from the dust;

Swirls and twirls them all around,
children chase them down a street,
until the wind has lost all its steam,
and the wilted leaves settle down.

Streets are now blanketed in white,
icicles hang from the limbs of trees,
homes and trees decked with lights,
Christmas is knocking on the door.

Jingle Bell carols lighten our hearts,
Santa welcomes us all at the stores,
will come down chimneys tonight,
leave gifts for all to their delight.

Garden Of Life

Snake Plant

A yellow-fringed plant with tall plumb leaves,
in the florist's arched window caught her eye,
as if by some magic spell lured her to the store,
Sansevieria Trifasciata, Snake Plant, label bore.

In a terracotta planter, it went to its new home,
florist had said it belonged to the cactus family,
not thirsty, needs little sunlight and little care,
removes bad energy, cleans toxins in the air.

She gave it some loving care, hummed along,
cleaned its long leaves with white damp cloth,
spotted a deep gash across the veins of a leaf,
rubbed its wound gently to give it some relief.

A few months of nurture and the plant grew,
in time, to her surprise, her asthma improved;
she went to the florist to buy a larger clay pot,
who sold her a fancy one from the garden lot.

She repotted the plant and added more soil,
gave *Feng Shui* touch, good *chi* to her room,
by a window she placed it for morning light,
then she slept like a baby, night after night.

A World Without Art

Imagine a world without art:
No frescos at Sistine Chapel,
No Michelangelo, no Gustav,
No Da Vinci's Mona Lisa,
No Picasso's sad clown,
No Rembrandt, no Renoir,
No museums in France.

We would indulge in idle talk,
over bread, wine and cheese,
until the late hours of evening.

Imagine a world without art:
No Manet's Spanish Singer,
No Degas' Russian Dancers,
No Van Gogh's blue Irises,
No Pissaro's Haymakers,
No Monet's footbridge over
Water lily pond at Giverny.

We would play a game of chess,
claim pawns, knights and queen,
until the night morphs to dawn.

Garden Of Life

Imagine a world without art:
No Beatles to cheer our hearts,
No reruns of Casablanca,
No Beethoven, no Mozart,
No waltzing to Strauss,
No old jukebox playing
Our favorite Sinatra song.

We would live robotic lives,
no inspiration to draw upon,
from dawn to dawn.

Dying River

Five of the world's mightiest rivers of Asia are dying:
China's Yangtze, Myanmar's Salween, Pakistan's Indus,
Mekong, the longest river that snakes through East Asia,
and the sacred Ganges River of my old country, India.

Once upon a time, people died of old age and diseases,
today, it is cancer, thanks to those who chop down trees,
pollute our earth, the water we drink, and air we breathe,
where industrial revolution has taken over agrarian land.

From the foothills of the Himalayas, flows the Ganges,
into the holy town of Rishikesh, where devout pilgrims
in saffron wraps sit in lotus position, chanting mantras;
millions flock here each year for a spiritual awakening.

Hindus cleanse their sins with a dip in the blessed river;
hermits with shaven heads, orange garb and long beards,
who have renounced the world, meditate with holy beads;
ashes of the departed emptied into the river for salvation.

Chemicals and human waste float down the holy river,
as the faithful chant, float clay oil lamps, toss marigolds
and roses, offer coconut and milk to Goddess Ganga,
then take home the toxic water for loved ones to drink.

Garden Of Life

A Bird's Call

Hark, hark, the blackbird cried.
    You have a message for me?

Hark, hark, it's a beautiful day.
    Sing that to the world, birdie.

Hark, hark, saw a lovely parade.
    Happy days are here, birdie.

Hark, hark, I shall sing for peace.
    You're wise, my flying friend.

Hark, hark, I can barely breathe.
    Why so, dear winged friend?

Hark, hark, brush fire out there.
    Stay here on the porch, birdie.

I must now fly back to my nest,
In the shade of trees where I can rest.

Garden Of Life

Come Dance With Me

Today, I am teaching
my daughter's poodle to dance;
he loves music,
perhaps, he loves to dance.
I lift his front paws,
he stands on his hind legs,
we do the Salsa,
his feet in tune,
one-two, one-two,
while the music plays on.
Good boy, you can dance,
I say to him;
he then sits beside me,
his beady black eyes
looking up at me;
I think he wants to dance again.
I think he wants to Rock-n-Roll tonight.
I love to Cha-cha
makes me feel light-hearted,
young again.

Garden Of Life

How about you?
No dance partner?
No problem;
Got a preference?
Go solo,
twist your way,
through the grocery aisles;
strike a pose,
sashay your neck,
do the Bharat Natyam.
Group dance, anyone?
Go on, twirl around,
do the Sufi dance;
slip on your grass skirt,
lei around your neck,
do the Hula;
put on your dancing shoes,
dance on the streets,
if you must,
but, please dance.

Garden Of Life

Torch of Harmony

Alas, how we have plunged
into a sea of invisible walls
between the young and old;
that old silly power struggle
between a man and woman,

that mighty yawning divide,
between the rich and poor,
the politics of race and color,
that only intend to divide us;
let us come together in peace,

pipe sweet music for humanity,
like the songbirds in the trees,
yellow daffodils on city streets,
those graceful white calla lilies,
blooming by the silvery stream;

the lovely cherry pink blossoms,
and white flowering dogwoods,
tall pines and ancient redwoods,
stately oak, and spiritual banyan,
animals thrive in such harmony.

America 2020

The Invisible Enemy, Covid-19

U.S economy was booming, unemployment rapidly falling, wages were rising, people were thriving, when all at once Corona leaked form a Wuhan lab, crept upon us in the dark, like a serpent in the grass, held us hostage in our dwellings.

US-China travel halted—some reports said the deadly virus came from a horseshoe bat, sold at a wet market in Huanan, Batwoman Shi Zhengli said it came from bat cave in Yunnan, many said, virus manmade at Wuhan lab...How do we know?

Whistleblower Dr. Li Wenliang told us so, virus is contagious, Li arrested for spreading rumors, died soon after of the virus, Huang Yan Ling, lab worker, alleged 'patient zero,' vanished, China said all was fine, reports revealed thousands had died.

As Chinese New Year neared, travel restraints were imposed, domestic travel was banned, so the locals ventured offshore, Beijing and other cities on a lockdown, festivities cancelled; boarded shops, empty streets, Wuhan became a ghost town.

Garden Of Life

Yet, five million Chinese shopped and dined in South Korea,
Japan, Thailand, Italy, Spain and unwittingly spread the virus;
Italy was the hardest hit, Europeans were rattled—thankfully,
U.S. travel ban from China and Europe averted an early crisis.

Whistleblower Dr. Ai Fen went missing, evidence destroyed,
after she told '60 Minutes Australia' that virus was infectious,
citizen journalists—Li Zehua, Fang Bin, Chen Quishi arrested,
but who was there to tell, foreign journalists were all expelled.

Panic set in, America stocked up on groceries and provisions;
schools, restaurants, bars shut down, public events cancelled,
citizens ordered to stay at home, church masses also banned,
life came to a grinding halt, telecommuting became the norm.

Tens of thousands died worldwide, economy took a nosedive,
Prez. Trump accused China of mishandling virus and raw data,
plotting with the WHO, keeping pandemic cloaked in secrecy,
and withholding medical supplies in times of healthcare crisis.

Garden Of Life

China warned it would cut off pharma supplies to the US, but this only emboldened President Trump, he urged companies to return and build manufacturing supply chain here at home, not be manipulated, or held hostage by a communist regime.

He summoned a task force of CEOs, scientists, and doctors, to set up test centers nationwide and develop treatment plans; America must return to work, people are hard-pressed he said, lockdowns had driven many to drugs, depression, and suicide.

Alas, Charlatans hoarded supplies, sold them at inflated price, president invoked Defense Production Act, asked companies to mass-produce protective equipment, so frontline workers were shielded, and hospitals increased stockpile of essentials.

With no therapeutics available, ventilators became the lifeline, handwashing, social distancing, face masks became the norm; recovered patients donated plasma, to help the others mend, manufacturers rose to the occasion, to help build up reserves.

Garden Of Life

In New York City, men in white hazmat suits moved bodies to
makeshift morgues, such were the stories that made headlines;
retired doctors, nurses, first responders came out to volunteer,
healthcare evolved in a flash, telemedicine sprouted all over.

Some governors returned recovering seniors to nursing homes,
a misstep that infected others, sent thousands to their deaths;
when situation turned grim, Mercy ships with helicopter decks
dispatched to the two coasts, to help with the patient overflow.

Sirens blaring, paramedics rushed patients to nearby hospitals,
with city dwellers dying at alarming rate, lockdowns enforced,
stores shuttered, streets deserted, virus isolated communities,
even struck tourists on cruise ships and military ships far at sea.

Nurses shed tears in the hallway, went to the rooftops to pray,
New Yorkers opened their hearts, doors, windows, in gratitude
they waved, clapped hands, made music on the pots and pans,
to pay tribute to healthcare workers, first responders, doctors.

Garden Of Life

Another day, another lifting scene: Blue Angels, Thunderbirds
zipped through the sky, to honor those who served and died,
in the line of duty, bystanders and police joined in the cheer;
a magical moment it was, they sang, saluted, raised high fives.

In New Orleans, Louisiana, Mardi Gras carnival drew crowds
of revelers to the streets, they drank and danced, tossed long
strings of bright beads to cheery fans, as fancy floats passed,
unaware an invisible enemy hovered among the merrymakers.

With extended lockdowns, spirits broken, and deep in debt,
jobless Americans protested, they wanted to return to work,
waited long hours in their cars, for boxes of food donations;
churches, food banks, and farms, stepped up in compassion.

Confined to virtual learning at home, struck by cabin fever,
come summer, when the sun was up, warm waters inviting,
the young and restless flocked to bars, bistros and beaches,
ignored social distancing rules, and the inevitable happened.

Garden Of Life

With the corona wave, two models emerged: one called for
extended lockdown, the other for back-to-school and work;
until, WHO Director called for a universal end to lockdown,
it had not worked anyplace, but wreaked havoc in our lives.

Broadway actor, Brian Mitchell, also played a cameo role;
he stood by his window, paid tribute to healthcare workers,
warmed the hearts of New Yorkers, as he sang in baritone,
The Impossible Dream from *Man of La Mancha* musical.

The pandemic roared into our lives like the eye of a storm,
knocked us off our two feet, turned our lives upside down,
stole loved ones from families, left behind broken dreams,
while politicians kept us under lockdown with an iron hand.

Austerity had driven many to poverty, hunger, and despair,
some committed suicide, others turned to spirits and drugs;
Trump's *Operation Warp Speed* gave us Covid-19 vaccine,
soon vaccine effect faded, did not work on the Delta variant.

Garden Of Life

Summer of Riots

On May 25, 2020, a 46-year-old black man
walked into a Minneapolis convenience store,
got something to eat with a $20 counterfeit bill;
police called, officer Derek Chauvin arrived,
handcuffed George Floyd,
walked him to the squad car,
but he resisted arrest—a struggle ensued,
Floyd went down on the blacktop.

Face down, he was pinned to the ground,
a white officer's knee on the nape of his neck,
nose bleeding, Floyd pleaded: *I cannot breathe*;
passersby begged officer Chauvin to stop,
but his knee pressed harder on the neck,
nine minutes later, paramedics arrived,
Floyd had no pulse, was rushed to ER,
too late, he had breathed his last.

That evening, Minneapolis black community,
led a peaceful march through the town,
next day, grief turned to violence when
Black Lives Matter and Antifa activists,
paid out-of-state protestors, anarchists,
and criminals released from prison,
joined the nationwide protests,
chanting: *No Justice, No Peace.*

Garden Of Life

Fellow officers who witnessed were discharged,
but that only sparked outrage and civil unrest;
rioters hurled Molotov cocktails and bricks
at law enforcement officers;
set a police precinct on fire,
and looted small businesses,
curfew imposed, to no avail,
nothing could bring George Floyd back again.

Meanwhile, in Missouri, David Dorn,
a 77-year-old black police chief,
was minding his friend's store,
when a black youth walked in,
grabbed some merchandise,
fatally shot the chief and fled,
yet no outrage among the blacks,
why did mainstream media ignore his death?

The same day, Captain David Patrick of California,
a black officer, also died in the line of duty,
yet, no call to honor his death;
but a counterfeit bill and Floyd's passing,
at the hands of a white police officer,
opened old wounds of racial divide,
led to breakdown in law and order,
left beautiful cities in ruins.

Garden Of Life

Urban guerilla warfare, fear, panic, everywhere,
by day, rioters went on a wild looting spree,
trashed and torched small businesses,
disguised by face masks,
they escaped in the dark,
while American cities burned.
Where were the cities' mayors?
Where was mainstream media?

On this last day of May, protests ignited at a park,
down the street from the DC White House,
rioters hurled bottles and bricks,
at the Secret Service police,
president rushed to the bunker;
and when the clock struck ten,
arsonists set fire to the basement,
of the historic St. John's Episcopal Church.

As the sun set, the House of worship burned,
protestors broke through the police line,
charged to the White House grounds,
target now within arm's reach,
but where was the park police,
where was the National Guard,
commissioned to protect
the president and the White House?

Garden Of Life

All at once, police in riot gear appeared,
pushed back at the rowdy rioters, with
tear gas, smoke bombs, pepper spray;
and when the clock struck eleven,
curfew went into effect,
army buses patrolled DC,
taking into police custody,
anyone roaming the streets.

Meanwhile, delayed curfew in New York City,
gave rioters license and time to vandalize and steal,
burn the city into the dark of the night,
mayor ordered police to stand down;
president warned he would send in
the National Guard, if the city
did not rein in the violence,
that plagued Democrat-run towns.

As the story unfurls, officer Chauvin charged
with second-degree murder of Floyd's death,
but the news did not please Black Lives Matter,
or local politicians, who supported the rioters,
they called to defund and disband the police,
even dismiss plain-clothes officers,
replace police training programs,
with social worker hiring programs.

Garden Of Life

Antifa anarchists, clad in all black and ski masks,
marched alongside Black Lives Matter,
they defaced historical monuments,
brought down old civil war statues;
these Marxists held America hostage,
wanted to overthrow US government;
a new civil war was brewing,
but is this any way to solve a problem?

Black Lives Matter used Floyd's death,
to reignite racial tensions;
demanded reparations for,
enslaved ancestors, eons past;
Atlanta on fire, Chicago looted,
many asked: Do only black lives matter?
What about white, brown, and blue lives—the police?
Truth is: All lives matter.

You may have heard of the land of OZ,
but have you heard of CHAZ and CHOP?
Welcome to Seattle, a hip vegan city in Washington,
one summer evening of 2020, Antifa anarchists
created a storm, planted their own flag,
on a downtown six-block plot of land,
called it CHAZ: *Capitol Hill Autonomous Zone*,
and dictated terms of engagement with the town.

Garden Of Life

CHAZ squatters claimed statehood,
demanded a say in the nation's policies;
they had no plans to leave, or surrender
the six-block land they had seized;
when Mayor Durkan was asked by press:
"How long do you think Seattle looks like this?"
"I don't know. We could have a summer of love,"
she replied, with a broad grin.

Here in the land of CHAZ,
occupiers were in a state of Nirvana:
food, artwork, and music in the air;
Summer of love? you ask,
oh no, they had a hidden agenda;
siege of Seattle was just the launch;
soon signs went up, barricades brought in,
traffic cordoned off from the occupied land.

Seattle residents signed a petition,
calling for Mayor Durkan to resign,
president threatened to send in the troops,
to protect US federal property;
CHAZ footprint reduced by half,
occupied land renamed CHOP:
Capitol Hill Occupied Protest;
squatters waved "Defund The Police" banners.

Garden Of Life

When two nights of burglaries and shootings,
led to the deaths of two black teenagers,
in the occupied land of CHOP,
Mayor Durkan asked the police,
to dismantle the occupied zone,
and reclaim the Seattle land;
then she walked back,
her *Summer of Love* comments.

Black Lives Matter then moved to DC,
settled at a park down from the White House,
named it BHAZ: *Black House Autonomous Zone*,
Mayor Bowser flexed her muscle,
commissioned the two-block 16th Street
be renamed: *Black Lives Matter Plaza NW*;
overnight, a big bold mural of the moniker,
was painted in deep yellow on the pedestrian walk.

President Trump signed an executive order,
warned anarchists they could face
ten-years in prison,
if they vandalized federal property;
soon, the ringleader and his band of hundred,
who plotted to topple bronze statue
of President Andrew Jackson in DC,
were arrested and taken into custody.

Garden Of Life

Elsewhere, rioters went on a rampage,
defaced, toppled historic statues of U.S. presidents:
George Washington, Abraham Lincoln,
Thomas Jefferson and Ulysses Grant,
Christopher Columbus, Robert E. Lee,
Francis Scott Key, even Mahatma Gandhi;
they forgot, history belongs to all Americans,
good or bad, it must be preserved.

Terror, terror everywhere, yet BLM called to ban police,
situation in Portland was by far the worst,
federal courthouse was set on fire,
when president sent in the troops,
angry mobs threatened
to blow up the courthouse,
with officers trapped inside,
violence rocked the city for a hundredth night.

Long after George Floyd was laid to rest,
the city of Kenosha was up in flames,
Floyd's death was just an excuse to
loot and burn America, label it racist,
turn it into a Marxist state,
rewrite history and the US Constitution;
a year later, officer Chauvin sentenced
to twenty-two and a half years in prison.

Garden Of Life

Tyranny, Be Not Proud

Yesterday, storm winds howled all over town,
today, the Orwellian world is on a lockdown,
schools closed, virtual Zoom classes a norm,
children depressed, church doors padlocked;

governors and mayors shut down restaurants,
bars, gyms, and the small businesses in town,
they wined and dined with friends, yet seized
business and liquor licenses of the little guys;

woke up one morning to a surveillance state,
where cancel culture stifled freedom of speech,
social media censored, silenced us so callously,
Marxists tyrannized, covertly rewrote history;

in the name of Corona, our civil rights trodden,
in the name of Corona, our dear freedoms lost,
lawmakers turned lawbreakers as cities burned,
and those in power turned against their people;

as one year of nightmare morphed to another,
Covid mandate paved way for Marxist regime,
and illegal migrants marched in, occupied U.S.
enemies within had sold our nation for a song;

as we waited for the dystopian tempest to pass,
with each passing week, our fears compounded,
until the oppressed rose, could take it no more,
Tyranny, be not proud, we are now awakened.

Do not blindly follow others; you may fall off the cliff in the fog.

Garden Of Life

Notes

Without You: Fictional poem showing opposites attract.

Kami Gods: Fictional poem woven around the January 1995 Kobe earthquake of Japan.

Chinese Matchmaker: Fictional poem woven around the tradition of arranged marriages in China, woven around the time of the Korean War (1950-1953) when Communist China supported North Korea against South Korea. The Chinese year of the Tora – Tiger – is considered a year of ill-omen to wed.

Garden of Life: Fictional poem about an autistic child. More than 3.5 million American children are autistic. They face many educational challenges.

Grandma's Tin Box: Fictional poem told in the spirit of Christmas giving. A grandmother teacher her grandson to give and share.

Poor Henry Chandler: Fictional poem prompted by news that doctors "in residency" work long hours to the point of fatigue.

In Search of Utopia: Fictional poem about two friends who run into each other one day. Over food and drinks, they have a philosophical discussion. "Utopia," an imaginary happy island, is a word coined by British philosopher and author, Thomas More. On the other hand, "dystopia" is an imaginary place or a society that is unhappy, where people live in fear, poverty, or under inhumane and oppressive conditions.

Mystery Envelope: Fictional poem.

Garden Of Life

Murphy's Clouds: Fictional Poem based on Murphy's Law: "Anything that can go wrong, will."

A Farm Song: Fictional poem woven around true events. This poem is dedicated to the farmers of India. According to statistics reported by Indian news media, from 1997–2007, some 350,000 farmers committed suicide, most of them cotton growers in the western region of Vidarbha, Maharashtra. The unofficial figure is close to half-a-million. Many crops failed before harvest, and they could not repay the farm loans taken from loan sharks, who charged exorbitant interest rates of 25 to 30 percent. In despair, the farmer drank lethal chemical pesticide and took his life. A pesticide meant to kill the weeds on his land. His family then inherited the farm, since the farm loan was taken only in his name. Bt Monsanto seeds were blamed for mass farmer suicides across India. Read more about it in my non-fiction book, "To India, with Tough Love." Chapter: The Lost Decade: Farmer Suicides."

The Tribal Doctor: True story. This poem is dedicated to Dr. Hanumappa Sudarshan – Padmashree & Mother Teresa award winner, a physician, social entrepreneur and tribal rights activist. He empowered the forest-dwelling Soliga tribe of Biligiriranga (B.R.) Hills in the southern state of Karnataka, India. While many tribal areas, along the eastern and central states of India, were infiltrated by Maoist-style communists, home-grown Naxalites, the doctor took measures to ensure B.R. Hills did not fall into communist hands. Hailed as their hero, he continued to live among the tribals. I met the doctor in October 2010. We were both speakers on a poverty panel at the Indiana State University. Read more about him in my non-fiction book, "To India, with Tough Love." Chapter: Good Samaritans.

Tutankhamen: Personal story. When my children were young, I took them one weekend to the Rosicrucian Egyptian Museum in San Jose, California, where we saw artifacts and mummies of ancient Egyptian leaders. From the gift shop, I purchased a coffee-table book of Tutankhamen, which I read to my children over and over again.

Sleep Thumbelina, Sleep: Fictional poem.

Garden Of Life

Everything Will Be OK: A true story about a barn sign I sometimes passed that became a source of inspiration.

A Distant Voice: Fictional poem. The jogger, who comes from a broken family, helps an old man who has suffered a stroke. In the process, his faith in humanity is restored and he is transformed.

Christmas Gift: Fictional poem. A widow discovers the men in her life were cheating on her. She realizes you don't need a man to be happy, as happiness comes from within. So, for Christmas she gets herself a little dog, who returns her love and is always there for her.

Thin-Skinned: Fictional poem about staying light-hearted in life, turning a deaf ear to the naysayers, and dancing our cares away.

Divine Scale: Fictional poem. All the money in the world cannot buy us a ticket to heaven, if we have lived a dishonorable life.

Seven Year Itch: Fictional poem. A woman who has given her all to her family, learns her husband has cheated on her.

Journey: Fictional poem based on how meditation can help heal cancer patients. It works in conjunction with the cancer treatment program. The medical treatment helps cure cancer, while the yoga-meditation program helps with the healing, potentially reducing the recurrence of cancer. Cancer healing Centers: The Chopra Center: Healing Cancer Though Mind-Body Medicine; American Cancer Society: Meditation; The Gawler Foundation: Cancer-healing Retreats.

Narcissist: Fictional poem based on research. Some narcissists may show signs of bipolar depression. They tend to be delusional, suffer from low self-esteem, and have a grandiose image of themselves. Thus they belittle others. Some of these traits have been woven through the threads of this poem.
Narcissism is a mental disorder and is more prevalent in males. It may be genetic or it can be traced back to a person's childhood or

adolescence, when he/she was perhaps abandoned, neglected, excessively criticized or pampered as a child.

In this poem, the protagonist craved for his father's love. With the passing of his father, that love was lost forever. Psychotherapy is helpful for those who suffer from this disorder, but symptoms can reappear when a person is under extreme stress.

Puffs: Fictional poem. A wife encourages her husband to quit smoking for the sake of his health, to no avail. She realizes the only way to get him to stop smoking is if she joined him when he smoked. Her strategy worked. He quit smoking, as he hated to see her puff and cough. Love can work in mysterious ways.

A Rewarding Life: Fictional poem. A disenchanted young lawyer, takes a life-changing journey to seek the truth in life. In the process, he finds himself. What he learns transforms him. It inspires him to give of himself. As a result, he dedicates the rest of his life to improve the lives of others.

The Salt March: aka Dandi March. Fictional story set in Ahmedabad, Gujarat – Mahatma Gandhi's home state. The tale is based on Mahatma Gandhi's 25-day, 241-mile non-violent *Salt March* held in March 1930, to protest against the British salt monopoly. Gandhi asked the Indians to make their own salt. For this civil disobedience act during the British Raj days of India, he and some 60,000 were arrested and jailed.

The First Buddha: Siddhartha Gautama Buddha: 623 – 543 BC. Poem is based on research. It narrates Buddha's life and teachings. Leaving behind a princely life, Buddha set out on his travels as a hermit – sanyasi. He sought the truth in life until he found enlightenment and became a Bodhisattva.

On his path to PariNirvana – total bliss – Buddha shared his knowledge with others. He believed that when we free ourselves of worldly desires and attachments, we are awakened and enlightened, and can thus uplift others from their own suffering.

The Four Noble Truths he preached are: 1) life is suffering, 2) the cause of suffering is temptation and attachment, 3) we can end suffering by lowering our expectations in life, and 4) meditation.

Garden Of Life

Buddha's eight-fold path to attain Nirvana include shunning temptation, aggression, ego, greed, hate, hope, fear and anger.

Lumbini, Buddha's birthplace, is located in the Himalayan region along the Nepal-India border. The town of Bodh Gaya where he traveled, Isipatana where he was enlightened, and Kushinagar where he attained PariNirvana – total bliss – are located in Uttar Pradesh, a northern state of India.

Never Too Old To Dream: A poem of inspiration. Live life. You have only have one life to live.

Woodstock & War: True events. It was U.S President Lyndon B. Johnson who decided to engage in Vietnam's civil war. The 1968 Tet Offensive in Saigon caught America off-guard, led to tens of thousands of U.S. casualties.

Under U.S. President Richard Nixon, the war expanded to Cambodia, and more troops were needed. So the U.S. government, aka Uncle Sam, introduced the draft system, under which almost 40,000 young men were enlisted for service each month. Names of nineteen to 25-year-olds were drawn at a lottery drawing. When the sons of the rich and politicians were drafted, it led to a quick withdrawal by America.

More than 1.3 million Vietnamese died during the civil war. Names of over 58,000 fallen Americans are carved on the Vietnam Veterans Memorial wall in Washington D.C.

Some U.S. forces were engaged in spraying Napalm "Agent Orange" to clear Vietnamese jungles, so as to track enemy movement from the air. These American forces later developed lung cancer from exposure to white phosphorous.

The Vietnam War began in 1959. The first U.S. combat marines arrived in Vietnam in March 1965. On January 27, 1973, with the signing of the Paris Peace Accord, the Vietnam War came to an end. It took another two years for all U.S. troops to return home. With the signing of the treaty, the U.S. stock market plunged; so did the war-driven economy.

The poem focuses on the events of 1969, the year I migrated from India. President Richard Nixon had just been sworn into office. The war had been on-going for years. This was also the year of the 3-day Woodstock Music Festival held in Bethel, New York, where musicians, high on drugs, sang songs of peace.

Garden Of Life

The Great American Tragedy: True story of September 11, 2001 Islamic terrorists attacks at the World Trade Center in New York City, the Pentagon in Washington DC, and in the skies of Pennsylvania. The mastermind of these attacks was al Qaeda leader, Osama bin Laden, who lived in the caves of Afghanistan.
October 7, 2001: Accompanied by U.K. allied forces, the U.S. launched an attack in Afghanistan, where Al Qaeda members trained for jihadi activities. NATO allies joined the coalition later.
May 2, 2011: U.S. Navy Seals killed Osama Bin Laden at a compound in Abbottabad, Pakistan. His body was buried at sea.

Ravages of War: True story about U.S. invasion of Iraq: March 19, 2003-Dec. 2011. President George W. Bush Jr. believed Iraq had chemicals of mass destruction. "The smoking gun that could come in the form of a mushroom cloud." Armed with misinformation, he invaded Iraq. But where was the mushroom cloud? Huffington Post, "Iraq Death Toll Reaches 500,000 Since Start Of U.S.-Led Invasion, New Study Says," Oct.15, 2013. In Nov. 2014, New York Times reported on the two-decade-old chemical weapons found in Iraq during post-war cleanup. "More Than 600 Reported Chemical Exposure in Iraq, Pentagon Acknowledges."

Papa, Make Bad War Go Away: Fictional poem. The Syrian civil war (2011-2019) resulted in over half a million deaths.

Don't Cry Wolf: Reflections on our engagement in wars.

Bury Your Weapons: Reflections on war and peace.

Enemy Within: Reflections on America. The Great Recession of late 2007 to early 2009 was almost as bad as the Great Depression years of the 1930s in America. This time, many Americans lost their jobs, not only due to the downturn in economy, but also to offshoring of American jobs. Some also lost their homes due to loan fraud by banks. While Americans were bleeding, big banks were bailed by the government, and CEOs took home exorbitant compensation. Economic gap between the rich and the poor widened. Middle-class almost disappeared. The country was run by Wall Street bankers and

Corporate America, whose lobbyists roamed the halls of Capitol Hill to influence the nation's policies. In January 2009, Barack Obama succeeded President George W. Bush, and the economy that was already in a fall, further plummeted.

Eye For An Eye: Reflections on war. Gandhi's philosophy on non-violence is even more relevant today.

Stain on American Tapestry: True story about Black History exhibits at the Atlanta History Center displayed in the first decade of the new millennium. The latter part of the poem relates to historic exhibits and videos I had seen at The King Center in Atlanta, and TV footage of the day the Confederate flag was brought down in South Carolina in 2016.
A Civil War (1861-1865) was waged by then-Republican President Abraham (Abe) Lincoln and his Union Army of the North, to bring an end to slavery in the South. Democrats, who were then in power in the South, were the primary slave-owners. In 1863, the Emancipation Proclamation was signed to abolish slavery. It took two years to make it happen. A century-and-a-half later, racial tensions still prevail in America. This time, it is the politicians who have created a racial divide in the country because of their own personal biases.

A New Tomorrow: Reflecting on our past mistakes and planning for a new tomorrow.

Rise America, Rise: Reflections on America. The State House bell of Pennsylvania was built in 1752. It later developed a crack. In the late 1830s, it was named Liberty Bell, a symbol of the anti-slavery movement, women's suffrage, and civil rights movement.

Live Life: An inspiring poem.

A Soldier's Story: This poem is dedicated to the war veterans of America. Although it is a fictitious account of a soldier's deployment to Iraq and his PTSD (Post Traumatic Stress Disorder) syndrome, many veterans suffer from it. There are some twenty veteran suicides every day, even today.

Garden Of Life

Love & Soup Kitchen: Fictional poem prompted by the 2007-2009 Great Recession of America. When the recession officially ended, multinational corporations fared well, but most did not hire American workers. They continued to outsource jobs offshore. It was a jobless economic recovery. Unemployment hovered around 10 percent. In reality, it was twice as high. Many stopped looking for jobs and returned to school to acquire new skills; some took jobs that paid a lot less, or had multiple jobs to put food on the table. Meanwhile, the stock market continued to soar, while disparity between the rich and the poor widened. Such disconnect continued between Wall Street and Main Street.

Hungry in New York City: Personal story of a day in 1969 in New York City. As a new arrival from India, I was touched to see a hungry man look for leftovers in a large trash bin in a rich America. The scene resonated with me. Today, the city is in ruins, highlighted by corruption in politics.

A Ray of Sunshine: True story as told to me by my daughter, who ran into Ray, a homeless man in New York City. Even though, at the time she had not much money to spare, as jobs were hard to come by, she gave what she could. It was during the Great Recession of America (late 2007-2009), caused by Wall Street greed.

Living High On Wall Street: True story. For long, cocaine and other drugs have been commonplace on Wall Street, even among bankers, CEOs, and executives, who have much influence in Congress.
A July 2012 Business Insider news article "Cracked Tales of Cocaine on Wall Street" reported, "former Bear Stearns CEO Jimmy Cayne allegedly kept an antacid bottle full of cocaine at his desk." Cayne was blamed for his firm's collapse during the 2007 financial crisis that led to the Great Recession of America in 2008-2009.

The Gambler: Fictional poem.

On Death Row: Fictional poem woven around the Texas death row procedures found on the internet. I used to be against death penalty, but with mass terrorist attacks in the past few years, my thoughts have changed.

Garden Of Life

Since the death penalty was re-instituted in 1976, Texas has executed more death-row inmates than any other U.S. state, with 561 executions through April 2019. The Polunsky Unit of Texas is a prison for death row inmates. In 2015, Virginia then ranked a distant second with 113 executions. Total executions in the U.S. from 1976 to April 2019 were 1,494. Source: Death Penalty Information Center, "Number of executions by state and region since 1976."

Jaws of Hell: True story told to me by a former foster mother, a representative of non-profit, Hope. The victim's name has been changed to maintain her privacy.

Human trafficking was a $30 billion-plus industry in the world in 2015. In America, it is a federal crime, punishable by up to 20 years in jail. Children in foster care and child welfare systems are the most vulnerable. In a 2013 nationwide raid across the country, 60 percent of sex trafficking victims rescued by the FBI were children from foster care homes. On April 22, 2015, the U.S. Senate finally passed the Human Trafficking bill. Foster parents are paid by the government for children's care. Many of these parents exploit the children by sex-trafficking them for extra money. Children all over the world are in jeopardy much more so today.

Huffington Post, "Stopping the Foster Care to Child Trafficking Pipeline," by Malika Saada Saar, Director at Rights4Girls, Special Counsel on Human Rights for the Raben Group, October 29, 2013; and Fostering Perspectives, Vol. 18, No. 2, May 2014 issue, "Human Trafficking: What Foster Parents Should Know." CAS Research & Education, "FactSheet: Foster Care and Human Trafficking."

Flying Trapeze: Fictional poem woven around real life scenarios. Young girls from India and Nepal are often abducted and sold into sex slavery or to traveling circuses across state lines in India.

Escape from Fate: Fictional poem woven around real life stories in India, where many young poor girls are kidnapped and forced into sex slavery. Sex trafficking is prevalent across the world.

Trail of Tears – Fictional poem woven around two diamond mining fields in West Africa – Sierra Leone and Zimbabwe – where children and bonded labor are used, and are physically and mentally abused.

Garden Of Life

Blood Diamonds: Civil War of Sierra Leone: 1991-2002. Conflict diamonds were traded by Revolutionary United Front rebels of Sierra Leone for weapons with Charles Taylor, former president of Liberia, who supported the insurgency in Sierra Leone. Diamonds mined in war zones are now banned by the UN. But mines in Zimbabwe and other African countries still employ children.

Curio Cabinet: Personal story of the things that were in the curio cabinet at my childhood home in Bombay—Mumbai of today.

Those Good Old Days: Ruminating over my childhood days during the 1950s and 60s in Bombay (Mumbai), India.

Ode to My Brother: Personal story of my family.

The Roads I Traveled: Personal story of my migration from India to America in early 1969. People in India used to say the roads of America are paved with gold, synonymous with the phrase "The Yellow Brick Road." What I found over the years, is a pound of knowledge of this world. Taoists say knowledge is worth a pound of gold. In that sense, I have found what I have been looking for.

Don't Let Life Pass You By: Thoughts to share.

Pearls of Life: Thoughts to share.

Footprints in the Sand: Thoughts to share.

Field of Shamrocks: Thoughts to share.

House of Light: Thoughts to share.

Sunset at Goa Beach: Winter vacation with husband in Goa, India.

The Waves: Thoughts to share.

Summer in The Adirondacks: Family vacations, upstate New York.

Garden Of Life

As The Seasons Turn: A child's growing years through the four seasons. A tribute to our beautiful nature.

God's Palette: A tribute to our beautiful nature.

Snake Plant: Fictional poem. A Chinese lady once suggested I buy snake plants for our home to remove bad chi (bad energy) and toxins in the air. It will also help you sleep better, she said. I took her advice. The plant recommended by NASA to naturally purify the air, also accompanies astronauts traveling in space.

A World Without Art: A tribute to all forms of art.

Dying River: Rivers are polluted by thoughtless acts of mankind.

A Bird's Call: A poem to share about a blackbird.

Come Dance With Me: True personal story. During the summer of 2015, I taught my daughter's little poodle to dance.

Torch of Harmony: Tribute to our beautiful nature.

The Invisible Enemy: True poem on Coronavirus—COVID-19—a virus that spread worldwide and killed millions. Research based on multiple sources.

Summer of Riots: True story of George Floyd's passing and the 2020 summer riots in America, instigated by Marxists—Black Lives Matter and Antifa activists—who wanted to take down the U.S. government.

Tyranny, Be Not Proud: True story. The year 2020 was a very dark year. First came the cancel culture, then came COVID-19. Next, we were held hostage to a summer-long of Marxist riots. Much of the year, people, businesses, schools were under lockdown. As one year morphed to another, millions of illegal immigrants from all over the world crossed the Mexican border into the U.S. since President Biden's Marxist agenda included open borders.

Made in the USA
Columbia, SC
19 June 2023